D1330615

Inspiring
FAITH
COMMUNITIES

a programme of evangelisation

MICHAEL HURLEY

Published by Messenger Publications, 2020
Copyright © Michael Hurley, 2020

ISBN 9781788122696

Designed by Messenger Publications Design Department
Cover Image: Solomnikov / Shutterstock
Typeset in Adobe Caslon Pro & Bernhard Modern
Printed by Hussar Books

Messenger Publications,
37 Leeson Place, Dublin D02 E5V0
www.messenger.ie

CONTENTS

Abbreviations

AA: Vatican II, *Apostolicam Actuositatem. Decree on the Apostolate of Lay People* (18 November 1965).

AGD: Vatican II, *Ad Gentes Divinitus. Decree on the Church's Missionary Activity* (7 December 1965).

CCC: *Catechism of the Catholic Church* (Dublin: Veritas, 1994).

CL: Pope Saint John Paul II, *Christifideles Laici, The Vocation and the Mission of the Lay Faithful* (30 December 1988).

EG: Pope Francis, *Evangelii Gaudium, The Joy of the Gospel, Apostolic Exhortation on the Proclamation of the Gospel in Today's World* (24 November 2013), 280.

EN: Pope Paul VI, *Evangelii Nuntiandi, Apostolic Exhortation on Evangelisation in the Modern World* (8 December 1975).

NMI: Pope Saint John Paul II, *Novo Millennio Ineunte, Apostolic Letter at the Beginning of the New Millennium* (6 January 2001), 40.

RM: Pope Saint John Paul II, *Redemptoris Missio, The Mission of Christ the Redeemer* (7 December 1990), 3.

Introduction

FOR A number of reasons, I deliberately chose *Inspiring Faith Communities* as the title of this book. Firstly, I find the idea of life as a journey very appealing. I like to think of myself as being on a journey that is unique and rich in meaning, even if greatly insignificant in terms of world, or even local, history. I also suspect that at times during life many people become acutely aware of their own unique journey, which may call them to freedom and to take responsibility for their own choices and decisions. The decisions then taken will, in turn, shape the type of people they become.

Secondly, in recent years, I have become ever more aware that Jesus Christ, as the ground and purpose of my being, seeks to engage me in a deeply personal and tender way so that I may know freedom as his gift to me. In John's Gospel he reveals whom he wishes to be for me: 'I am the way, the truth and the life' (Jn 14:6). He seeks to be my path, fulfilment and healing, and the way to peace among all peoples. Thus, if I remain apathetic or agnostic before him I set aside his path towards my authentic freedom, and risk following my own wishes. Pope Francis explains that the experience of greatest freedom is found when an individual allows his or her life to be guided by the Holy Spirit who 'knows well what is needed in every time and place. This is what it means to be mysteriously fruitful'.[1]

Thirdly, I choose the title for my book in the hope that God may use its pages so that you, as reader, will know more deeply the freedom to which you are called. My hope then becomes that through you other people will come to live with joyful freedom.

1   *EG*, 280.

It is now almost twenty years since I witnessed the publication of my first book, *Transforming Your Parish*.[2] In it, I made available some of what I was learning at that time about the renewal of parish life. I described a series of five presentations to initiate such a process by leading participants to understand the importance of evangelisation. More importantly, I outlined a practical method to help them share faith within their homes, streets and places of work and leisure. The series sought to deepen, for participants, their sense of God, and give them an experience of community. My thinking was simply that there can be no true evangelisation without personal conviction and conversion.

A number of influences have led me to conclude that now may be an opportune time to recast and update what I had written. The first is the feedback I received from individuals and parish leaders, which communicated the personal and communal impact of the programme, as well as their suggestions towards enhancing the quality of outline and presentation. In this respect I am deeply grateful to feedback from many parts of Ireland, as well as from parishes in England, Malta, the US, Australia and Africa, which adapted the programme to their own local situations and culture. The second is that much has been written and debated during recent decades that have brought evangelisation and the place of parish renewal into focus. As my humble contribution, I wish here to offer what I have seen to be of benefit towards parish evangelisation. The third influence arises from my observation that changes in expectations, atmosphere and dynamics during that time must be accommodated for effective community and voluntary learning to take place. Today, the best didactic processes include attention to welcome and hospitality, with greater participation and interaction among participants, and with their presenter.

Inspiring Faith Communities reflects feedback I have received; an increasing focus on parish and evangelisation; and changed emphases

2   Michael Hurley, *Transforming Your Parish*, Dublin: Columba Press, 1998.

on best practices in educating and learning. At the same time, this book has grown from what I have seen works well in local parish and community groups. The programme that I describe here has already been employed by a wide number of parishes from diverse socio-economic backgrounds. Some recent feedback suggests that it has facilitated for participants newness in relating to the person of Jesus Christ, and a new vision for parishes. It has left some people wanting 'more' and asking 'What happens next?' For this reason, it has been a catalyst for the launch of new ministries. It is an ideal starting point for parishes that plan to set up small evangelising groups or 'parish cells'.

New Features
There are a number of new features in *Inspiring Faith Communities*. Presentations and meetings, for example, are described in much more informal and less structured terms that in *Transforming Your Parish*. This is achieved mainly through simplifying the outline of each meeting with three major sections: presentation on the theme; conversation over tea and coffee; and discussion, with reflection, to facilitate the assimilation, in personal terms, of the theme presented.

The first presentation focuses on faith and God's love rather than on transition, as in the previous book. The thinking behind this is that twenty years ago the necessity of change on the part of people of faith was still debated. Today, we see transition in almost every facet of life and so our question becomes more about how we can manage change and find meeting points with the God of wisdom during times of enormous transition.

I include a sixth presentation in this book. The theme of 'Jesus', as the second meeting, is now added. Twenty years ago, we made assumptions that the majority of Irish people either knew him in a personal way or at least had a framework of thinking and of expressing who he was. Today, there appears to be great lack of clarity about who he is, why he came and what he achieved.

The directions for each meeting, together with the prayer and reflection, are also greatly simplified. Indeed, the invitation to prayer and reflection together arises primarily from within the smaller discussion groups where people's readiness to pray in this way is more readily assessed. In addition, the emphasis is no longer on addressing pre-set questions but on having a good discussion in response to the presentation and on engaging together on issues of faith that are important to the participants.

Behind the planning and thinking of this book is one great story, namely, that of individuals and communities who, in their sensitivity to the Spirit of God, are learning to put new evangelisation on their agendas. As they do so, they come face to face with the surprises of God as he meets them in ways beyond their expectations. At the same time, they encounter obstacles, difficulties and resistances to the spread of God's word. This book reflects their experiences and, in turn, intends to support all who seek to lead others towards the experience of the Kingdom of God, of Jesus Christ among them, by offering some key sightlines and resources to assist them.

A companion booklet, *Living Word*, is published along with this book, for use by participants on each day of the programme. It introduces people to the use of scripture as a basis of prayer and facilitates a commitment to God.

Looking Ahead

I suggest that you read this book right through before making a decision to host, or not, the programme it describes. In this way, you will have an overview of the thinking that inspires it, of the dynamics and spirituality that best contribute to its success, and of possibilities for follow-up in your local situation. As you read, your reasons for hosting the programme are likely to become clear, and you are also likely to spot possibilities that will maximise its benefits in your local area.

The series of presentations, as recorded here, are given by way of offering general guidelines and resources. They are not to be followed slavishly. I have already seen the programme greatly blessed in many different settings. It seems to work best when a few people, or indeed an individual, are inspired to reach out to others in their parish community, and who see in these pages a way to communicate information and, most crucially, a living faith. These people then gather a few others around them to form a guiding team to discern how best to host, advertise and run the programme.

I continue to be encouraged by the feedback people give me and to hear of their efforts and difficulties as they launch something 'new' in their parishes. They tell me of their apprehensions as they take it on. Many wonder whether they will have the resources and energy to see it through. At times, they are fearful about negative responses of fellow parishioners towards them and to what they propose. At times, too, they are afraid that their suggestions might not find the support of parish leadership, and may even be quashed from the outset. I equally hear of people's delight as the programme unfolds and as they see a sense of community form and hear others tell them what such a forum has meant to them, where they could ask questions and share their faith. As one person declared, 'I was so surprised at how much happened during the first two weeks that I decided to relax and see God at work in this way.'

I approach this writing with a number of convictions, which give focus to the series of presentations described here. These can equally be called my assumptions, which underpin what I write. The first is that God calls each of us to mission and to service, and then, in following his desires, he leads us to authentic freedom. He has so much to give us and desires that we live as free people, with responsible action, self-determination and confidence. A second underpinning conviction is that every baptised Christian is called to evangelise. God calls us to serve one another and to reach out beyond ourselves to the world. He wishes that we live and proclaim his name, through our actions and words, in a way that enriches those whom we meet, and that expresses our love for them. Thirdly, we are called to contribute towards parish renewal. In theological and pastoral thinking, the parish is an important entity in the renewal of God's people. It is a place where God dwells among his people, and where we are enriched in our worship and in our encounters with him. It is a place of communion with brothers and sisters, which we live out in being communities within our parochial community.

The programme described in these pages is ideal for those who are unsure about the basics of their faith and even about where they stand in relation to God. I have three hopes. Firstly, that it may help people take hold of their dignity and their freedom in Christ. Secondly, and as a consequence, that people will share their resources, and especially their faith, with others in a way that invites others to true freedom. Thirdly, that it will contribute to parishes becoming centres of new life and evangelisation.

In the following chapters, I will elaborate on each of my convictions, which underpin and link the presentations. I hope this will lead to a greater understanding of the background, inspirations and possibilities of the programme described.

Chapter 1

Called to Serve ~ A Personal Note

UNTIL my mid-teenage years, there was very little to suggest that life in the priesthood was for me. There was no priestly ancestry within my extended family, apart from one grand-uncle who ministered in the US. God was scarcely ever spoken about at home or in social conversations. At the same time, faith was in the atmosphere in which I grew up. Sunday mass, regular confession and some formal family prayer, normally the Rosary, were accepted as part of life. I took them for granted. I saw them as part of who I was, and of who we were as a family and as parish. For all the lack of personal engagement, they gathered us together as a parish community, brought us to our knees as a family, and provided a space for reflection as individuals.

Simple Events Awaken New Horizons
Then, one day when I was almost sixteen, as I cycled happily through the countryside, I experienced what I now describe as 'a surge of generosity'. It may have been due to the spirit of transition and the idealism of the 1960s. Perhaps it's a normal part of every young person's growth. Perhaps it reflects the good Junior Examination results I had received a few days earlier. All I know is that in that one instant I knew I wanted to do something worthwhile with my life. I wanted to make a difference. As I experienced it, it seemed to have little to do with God or religion. The impulse remained. I came to observe the life and work of a local priest. I witnessed the extent to which he was prepared to serve others, particularly the poor and the weak. Somewhere in my

mind I made a connection. I wanted to make a difference through life as a priest.

During the following two years, I was far from convinced that I would survive seven years of seminary preparation. I also knew I could leave at any time. However, the initial impulse and attraction were to shape much of the rest of my life. It led me to seminary life in Dublin. It was to be my first trip beyond Cork. As I now reflect, I see it as a divine appointment, as God's way of speaking to me in a way that I could understand at that time. I now interpret it as an intervention of grace. I felt called to serve the poor.

Another simple event, about eighteen months after I had been ordained, also had a profound impact on me. My first appointment included teaching and, at the same time, running a youth club for boys in Dublin's inner city. Many of the boys appeared to be vulnerable and at risk. I found this experience stressful, and it led to much dissatisfaction and analysis on my part. I began to question my work and emphasis as a priest. I deemed that what I was doing was not changing anything for the boys I had come to know. I happened to pick up *Bury Me in My Boots* by Sally Trench, in which she described her work among the deprived and homeless in London. At times it overtaxed her. Then, one day, as she lay confined to her bed from exhaustion and breakdown, she realised that her life had been spent working for God. She now knew her calling was to work with God. I was reading cold print on a page. But what an impact! The harvester has to wait for the rhythm of nature. I too need to work with the rhythm of God's plan for my life. I need to come to know him, and work with him, and not only for him. I recognised that I had been making a fundamental mistake in that I had seen my work as work for a distant God.

I began to read every spiritual book I could find. Scripture was no longer a textbook, but a living word. I began to speak very tentatively, at first, about my new-found interest. I was invited to my first Charismatic prayer meeting. I was somewhat confused by the spontaneity of praise and prayer. Praying in tongues made no sense to me. I even felt a bit frightened. I was intrigued at how people could get so much from a biblical reading. I was made somewhat ill at ease by the warmth with which people greeted one another. I went through much soul-searching in my attempt to integrate what I was now experiencing with what I already knew. I was not too sure that I would succeed. But something kept drawing me. It all took up to eighteen months.

I had no dramatic moment of conversion, only the gradual yielding to the Spirit of God, as I gradually gave him more and more permission to work in his way in and through me. I came to recognise that all I had been taught and knew intellectually was gradually taking on a new importance for me, and revealing my richness as a baptised person. I came to know that I was a child of God, and loved by him. A real friendship and relationship with Christ developed for me. I knew he was again calling me. This greatly shaped my emphasis in ministry. I simply wanted to tell others about what I was experiencing. My hope in doing so was to bring good news to the poor who would then come to know Christ's love for them, and the happiness and freedom he gives. For me, at that time, 'poor' referred primarily to those for whom God was a distant figure and who lived as if he did not exist. I began to trust the Spirit of God to use me beyond my inadequacies and poverty.

Living a New Call

In 1989, a further, and seemingly chance event was again to give me a new direction in life. I had occasion to hear a ten-minute input from Don PiGi Perini. He spoke about the work of evangelisation and the dramatic growth in faith, community and numbers that was taking place through cell groups in his parish at Sant'Eustorgio in Milan. Something in what he said appealed deeply to me, although he communicated in broken English, which I found difficult. For months I struggled with what I saw as a new vision for parish renewal.

I spoke to people, including friends, the local bishop and the parish priest. I eventually came to a time of personal decision: to accept a new vision for parish evangelisation and renewal, or to continue living priesthood as I had known it.

In May 1990, I arranged a visit to Sant'Eustorgio with three parishioners from the parish of St John the Evangelist, Ballinteer, Dublin. The occasion was the First European Workshop on the Parish Cell System of Evangelisation. This event challenged us but, equally, filled us with enthusiasm and possibilities for a new pastoral vision. On our return, we sought to interpret our experience of cell communities in terms of what we saw as pastoral challenges for our parish at that time. Within three years, thirty-one cell communities existed in Ballinteer, which meant more than 300 parishioners engaged in daily evangelisation. In the intervening years, many Irish parishes have adopted this method of renewal and evangelisation. A cell is a community of between four and twelve people, committed to evangelisation and to multiplying itself.

I now understand that what I heard in 1989 was a graced moment. I see it as God calling me to evangelise, and to do so in a specific way. It revealed a strategy for parish renewal in very concrete terms. It involved bringing people together in small communities, providing formation and pointing them towards mission within their networks of relationships of family, neighbours, work and leisure colleagues. In more technical terms, it meant establishing schools of prayer, which provide ongoing formation in faith and evangelisation throughout a parish, and a model of parish renewal as a community of communities.

I have named what I see as three personal and influential moments of grace. I interpret each as an occasion of God's call to me. I regret that I have not always lived them fully, with the courage and boldness that I could have. At times, I experienced anxiety and struggle in living them out. More importantly, they communicated to me the sense that, through divine interventions, I was living out what is my true self in God, and I knew a deep freedom in the service of others.

Fundamentally then, I remain deeply grateful. The experience of these three moments, which I recognise as God's call to friendship and freedom in the service of the poor; to evangelisation as my lived and spoken response about whom I knew; and to a new vision of parish renewal, provides the convictions and assumptions that underpin the series of presentations described below. Their echo permeates each presentation.

Daniel Berrigan, an American Jesuit priest and 1960s anti-war and anti-draft activist, poet, pacifist and educationist, claimed that the best way to make the future different is to live the present differently. Today, the Western world lives through great transitions. The Christian message is often ignored, silenced and derided, and Christians at times feel persecuted because they profess to follow Jesus Christ. Equally, it is within this culture that God seeks our faithfulness, enthusiam and conviction. The myriad events of each day's unfolding remain the opportunities where he reveals himself to us. Here we learn to embrace daily crosses and know that they also carry the seeds of resurrection and of new life. As we tap into the mystery of his life and love in the silence of our hearts, we hear him, and know his transforming power at work. He leads us to daily worship with brothers and sisters, and to look together beyond ourselves to reach out to all as good news for the poor. He invites us to bloom where we are planted, with his Spirit as our guide and wisdom. All the time there are moments of grace, of small 'chance' events, when he points us to new directions and horizons, and to what our families and parishes can be. It is his initiative. It is all his work. In this way, too, the seeds of a new future are being planted.

In the following chapters, I reflect further on what I identify above as God's call to friendship that frees us, to evangelisation and to a vision of parish renewal. I do so because of their significance for me, and, more importantly, to offer you, as reader, the opportunity to think about possible 'chance' events in your life as indications of what God may be inviting you to be and/or to undertake.

Chapter 2

God's Call

'THERE is no greater freedom than that of allowing oneself to be guided by the Holy Spirit ... and letting him enlighten, guide and direct us.'[3]

The first conviction that gives direction to the series of presentations in this book is that God calls us to a path that leads to freedom. Hearing his voice and living his call leads us to personal healing and transformation. I understand that to be human is to be restless and to be forever engaged in a quest for vision and purpose in life when we can live without anxiety and fear, and with tolerance and acceptance as we relate to all people. At its core, the Christian conviction is that when we know the Lord and allow his Spirit to guide us we become truly free.

Many examples in the scriptures tell of God calling individuals to undertake something new. These are presented as invitations of God's initiative. God intervenes. He invites a response. He calls people to dialogue, friendship and trust in him. For some, he then calls to dramatic action; at other times to a gentle response. At times the call is to leave one's country and one's people; at other times it means to return to one's own people.

I now take a very brief look at the dynamics of this divine initiative and the human response, largely by looking at the call of Moses, with particular reference to Exodus chapters three and four. Here we see God calling Moses to have a deep trust in the directions he gives for his life and for his people.

3   *EG*, 280.

Call of Moses

Moses became aware of the burning bush. He wanted to draw close to it and examine it. Then God spoke to him. He asked him not to come any closer but to take off his sandals because he was on holy ground. 'And Moses hid his face, for he was afraid to look at God' (Ex 3:6). God takes the initiative. He invites Moses to go to Pharaoh and bring God's people, the Israelites, to freedom out of Egypt. This call disturbs Moses. He is filled with apprehension at the enormity of the task and knows that it is beyond him to achieve. He objects to God. He pleads with him and issues a great outburst: 'Who am I that I should go to Pharaoh?' (Ex 3:11). God simply assures him, 'I will be with you', and gives him a sign of his presence.

Moses continues to doubt. He complains that in following God's invitation, the Israelites will be very sceptical about him and will ask him many questions that he will not be able to answer. What is he to say, for example, when they ask him God's name? At this point, God instructs him. He tells him to go and simply say, 'I am has sent me to you. … the God of your ancestors, the God of Abraham, the God of Isaac, the God of Jacob, has sent me to you' (Ex 3:14–15). God again tells him to go; and further instructs him to gather the elders of Israel and tell them what God has told him and that he has asked him to lead the people to freedom, and to 'a land flowing wtith milk and honey' (Ex 3:17).

God tells Moses that he is to go to Pharaoh, accompanied by the elders, and tell him of their encounter with God. They are to ask Pharaoh for permission to go on a three-day journey in order to worship and offer sacrifice to God. God reminds him that Pharaoh will not let them go 'unless compelled by a mighty hand' (Ex 3:19). In this way, he is reminding Moses that difficulties will arise but that he will be with him to overcome them.

Moses, however, still remains filled with a sense of inferiority at the task ahead. He fears the reaction of the people of Israel. He presents his difficulty to God. He asks, 'But suppose they do not believe me or listen to me, but say "The Lord did not appear to you'" (Ex 4:1). God promises him that he will be with him and will support him with dramatic signs to convince the people.

Even still, Moses remains hesitant. He surfaces another personal difficulty. He reminds God that he has never been 'eloquent … I am a slow of speech and slow of tongue' (Ex 4:10). God remains faithful to Moses. He understands him. He again invites him to go, and assures him, 'I will be with your mouth and teach you what you are to speak' (Ex 4:12). Yet this still does not convince Moses. The enormity of the task continues to terrify him. At this stage, he feels he has had enough. He blurts out in haste, 'O my Lord, please send someone else' (Ex 4:13). He is firm in his refusal. He has come to a defining moment.

God has listened attentively to all the questionings and arguments of Moses. He has addressed each one seriously and assured Moses that he would always be at his side and would intervene, even in dramatic ways, as needed in order for him to carry out his mission. He now grows impatient with Moses' refusal. He knows that Moses is missing the point; that his emphasis is upon himself and on the effort that would be demanded of him, while he fails to understand that God is taking the initiative in revealing his presence and friendship, and sending him in his name and power to achieve this particular mission.

However, God makes one further approach in the hope that Moses will accept the divine origin of his mission. He speaks to Moses about Aaron, his brother, who at that time was coming to meet him. He assures Moses, 'I will be with your mouth and his mouth, and will teach you what you shall do. He indeed shall speak for you to the people; he shall serve as a mouth for you, and you shall serve as God for him. Take in your hand this staff, with which you shall perform the signs' (Ex 4:15–17). Moses has arrived at a turning point. This is his moment of conversion. For him, it occasions surrender to God whom he has come to know and trust.

From that moment, Moses begins to make plans. He is now deeply aware that God is calling him to lead the Israelites to freedom; that this is not of his making; and that God will see it to completion. He will now walk by faith in God. He will expect the revelation of God's glory as he leads the people, and as he follows the voice and calling of God. He has freely said 'yes' to God, who will fill him with confidence as he leads the people towards freedom, even beyond these complaints and hardships.

I have traced the initial stirrings in Moses of God calling him. His story carries similarities to other callings from God that have prominence in the scriptures, for example Isaiah, Jeremiah, Elijah, Mary, the mother of God, Zechariah and St Paul, even though called in very different places and for different purposes. Zechariah, for example, was in the temple (Luke 1:8–25). Then the angel Gabriel told him that his wife would bear a son who 'will turn many of the people of Israel to the Lord their God'. No doubt Zechariah was alarmed. He was afraid what this might mean for him. He was highly sceptical that such a promise would be fulfilled. He resisted. He complained to Gabriel, 'How will I know that this is so? I am an old man, and my wife is getting on in years.' He was struck dumb for his refusal to believe. This became for him a sign that God was with him, and that he was not to set limits on what God may wish to do. When his time of service in the temple was over, he went home and Elizabeth, his wife, conceived John the Baptist.

God Surprises

I conclude that when God calls, a number of human responses occur. God surprises. He calls when the person is not expecting him. He raises many questions for the hearer who tends to resist because of a sense of personal inadequacy and inferiority. He calls to friendship and closeness with himself, and to serve and lead people to freedom in a way that is beyond their human capacity. He invites in a way that is made to measure and spoken to the individual in the concrete circumstances of life. He remains present, assisting and patient, as the hearer questions and discerns what she or he is feeling and hearing. Acceptance is normally experienced with the promise that 'I am with you. I will bring my call to completion in and through you. What I want is your availability and "yes" at each stage. I will continue to surprise you. Walk by faith and see "greater works being performed"' (Jn 14:12). The observations I have made are equally true for the small and daily invitations of God, as each disciple listens to his voice, and for the fundamental and life-changing invitations to which I have referred.

The Christian conviction is that life as a disciple who hears and lives the call of God is the pathway to happiness and authentic freedom. We find this throughout the scriptures. Psalm 23 is a good example: 'The Lord is my shepherd, I shall not want ... he leads me beside still waters; he restores my soul' (Ps 23:1–3). St Paul tells us, 'Where the Spirit of the Lord is, there is freedom' (2 Cor 3:17).

The Truth Will Set You Free

The quest for and attainment of freedom is equally at the core of the Christian experience. Jesus drew attention to this after he had seen great numbers of people fail to grasp the significance of his teaching. He said, 'if you continue in my word, you are truly my disciples; and you will know the truth, and the truth will make you free' (Jn 8:31–32). In other words, he declared that a chain of events occurs as individuals invite him into their open hearts. Firstly, they become disciples. They sit down, as it were, to learn at his feet and give a home to his word. Secondly, they commit to him and see him as the Truth who leads them to see that, at their deepest level, they are loved and forgiven in him. Thirdly, God promises to be with them to lead others to the experience of freedom.

It appears that today, there exists a widespread wish, even a demand, for freedom. It is normally felt and explained as the desire for personal autonomy, authenticity and confidence. Freedom, thus understood, means seeking to live increasingly without the limitations of laws, traditions and values that are handed 'down'. At its extreme, it says, 'I am totally responsible for my own life, and can say and do what I like, without reference to another person or value'. Stated in this way, it carries the seeds of isolation and of life without community and commitment. Such a trend gives rise to contemporary debates about the fundamental meaning of freedom and its applications within the networks of family, work and leisure relationships. These debates are often emotional, direct and forceful because they lie at the heart of how we understand ourselves as individuals, and how we understand our local community and society. They are about what we do as free human beings, and how we can use our gift of freedom.

Pope Francis begins his apostolic exhortation, *Evangelii Gaudium*, by drawing attention to the source of freedom when he declares, 'The joy of the gospel fills the hearts and lives of all who encounter Jesus. Those who accept his offer of salvation are set free from sin, sorrow, inner emptiness and loneliness. With Christ joy is constantly born anew'.[4] It is important to note that freedom for him has two aspects. Firstly, it is a freedom to relate with and 'encounter' Christ at a deeply personal level. This brings fundamental changes, he says. Most notably people experience joy. Secondly, it is freedom from, in that it heals sin and selfishness, and assures a divine help and presence in times of 'sorrow, inner emptiness and loneliness'.

Scholastic teaching had already distinguished between 'freedom for' and 'freedom from'. The first identifies the purpose of freedom as the capacity for self-giving and surrender to love, generosity, altruism, moral codes and service. For the Christian, this path engages, through surrender, with the Father's love, and embraces his joy. The second challenges the perception of freedom as thinking and acting without restraints and moral inhibitions, and doing whatever one wishes. Such a path sets limits to our human potential and runs the risk of defining persons, events and possessions in terms of their

4   *EG*, 1.

22

usefulness and as means to personal comfort and peace, and with God seen as absent.

Depression vs Delight

Ronald Rolheiser, Oblate priest, speaker, columnist and author, has written widely about the inner world of the soul, and how we can nourish it. He claims that a chronic (as distinct from episodic) depression is a prevalent spiritual description of the Western world. In supporting his claim, he draws upon the stories people tell him about themselves. In this way he sees, for example, the prevalence of holding resentments, grudges and jealousies, and the fear of entering dialogue where hurt has been experienced. He notes the excuses that people give for their anger, which include having been hurt by a family member, Church representative or someone in authority. These excuses have the effect of limiting freedom in decision and action, yet people hold on to them, and have great difficulty in letting them go.

For Rolheiser, the opposite of chronic depression is delight. This is the felt sense of wonder when one knows the goodness of God, life, creation, friendships etc. It is the realisation that life has meaning and purpose. However, for Rolheiser, such moments are not encouraged within the climate of sadness in our Western culture. He understands that it is all the more important that these moments are fed and nourished by surrender to the issues of life and the awareness of God in the midst of all that exists. Paradoxically, he sees that happiness and freedom are realised only in giving them away.[5]

In biblical terms, to nourish our souls is to hear and keep God's word (Jn 14:23). This calls us to keep alive, cherish and give a place to the word of God in our hearts. It involves a surrender that will allow God's word to achieve what it says. It welcomes and savours the words of the Lord as true, and knows that in all the vicissitudes

---

5   Ronald Rolheiser, *The Shattered Lantern: Rediscovering a Felt Presence of God*, New York, NY: Crossroad, 1995; *Against an Infinite Horizon: the Finger of God in Our Everyday Lives*, New York, NY: Crossroad, 1995; *Forgotten Among the Lilies: Learning to Love Beyond Our Fears*, New York, NY: Doubleday 2007; *Wrestling with God: Finding Hope and Meaning in Our Daily Struggles to be Human*, Victoria: Image, 2018.

of living we are not alone: 'The Advocate, the Holy Spirit whom the Father will send in my name, will teach you everything, and remind you of all that I have said to you' (Jn 14:26). Even more fundamentally, God calls us into personal intimacy and dialogue with himself, as he teaches us who we truly are as individuals who are totally loved by him.

This is the path of discipleship, of learning at the feet of the Lord, while listening to the wind of the Spirit. It reveals who we fundamentally are. We come to know our dignity. This is God's way of revelation, and of taking up residence in our human hearts: 'We will come to them and make our home woth them' (Jn 14:23). This is not our success story. It is God's gift to us in our surrender as disciples. He assures us, 'my peace I give you … Do not let your hearts be troubled, and do not let them be afraid' (Jn 14:27). In these words, too, he assures us that behind the choppy waters of storms and the turbulence of living, dwells an inner peace that cannot be submerged against our wishes.

In hearing God's personal call to us, we know his Spirit, revealing the path that transforms us with ever-greater delight and freedom. His Spirit leads us on what can be an amazing journey when we know healing at the personal level of our spirit, mind and body, and our relationships. Healing, then, is the experience of freedom. It is felt as the acceptance of who we are as persons, with our weaknesses and strengths, while integrating and forgiving past hurts and false decisions. It is equally felt in belonging together as fellow disciples and pilgrims with all who follow Jesus and who are open in service to all humanity.

Chapter 3

Called to Evangelise

'WE HAVE been entrusted with a treasure, which makes us more human and helps us to lead a new life. There is nothing more precious we can give to others.'[6]

The second conviction underpinning this programme is that evangelisation is to be a primary focus for every Christian believer and parish. Without a direct and deliberate effort to open the core of faith to all people and share it in a way that enriches the quality of life of those encountered, many Catholic churches in the Western world will close, while, in their wake, small and largely disillusioned communities may survive (and perhaps only for a time). Hence, it is now more pastorally urgent than ever that we evaluate every pastoral activity of our parish and diocese in terms of their impact in animating a living faith for others.

The effort of evangelisation, for me, is not primarily about a return to parish and Church practices, and to the way things were in the past. The reality of our current cultural situation demands that we find new ways, and new courage, that reach beyond what we now do, and share what we know to be true in a way that is life-giving and that brings freedom. This presents the challenge to go deliberately beyond self, as individuals, parishes and Church, and inspire others towards Christ through the way we live and share the Christian experience.

Understood in this way, evangelisation means moving towards

6   *EG*, 264.

the fringes of the Church and of society, and in doing so adopting different approaches. It means moving towards all believers in a way that facilitates an ever-deepening experience of life in Christ. When people know an authentic relationship with Christ, they automatically want to tell their stories about him. They want to tell others about what brings them happiness and freedom. When it is not authentic, they tend to remain unsure and 'private' about what they believe, and reticent about publicly expressing it in their words and lifestyle.

Evangelisation also means moving towards those who were baptised but who do not worship with the Church, who do not live its values, or who have ceased to be Church affiliated. It involves engaging with people who have never known a personal conversion of faith to encourage them towards a freedom of 'allowing themselves to be guided by the Holy Spirit', and to send them as missionary disciples towards the fringes.

The Spread of Christianity
Evangelisation is as old as Christianity. The story of Jesus was passed on through the words and stories of those who had come to follow and believe in him. People did not come to believe in him until they heard of him 'And how are they to hear without someone to proclaim him? And how are they to proclaim him unless they are sent?' (Rom 10:14–15). From the outset, people heard his story. It connected with something within them. It attracted them. It made sense to them. They responded and welcomed it. They became his disciples and then, in turn, began to tell others about him.

Christianity spread as people shared with others how meeting Jesus had enriched them. No doubt they told the details of how, when and where their meeting with him happened. Everyday conversations then became the normal way that people came to believe in him.

The same remains true for us today. God normally deals with us in a very human way. He does not bypass the fact that we are social beings who learn from one another. We first hear the lived examples and stories of faith from another who stirs our Christian imagination at its beginnings. A parent, grandparent, friend or someone we trust is often our first influence. The opposite remains equally true, namely, that when the facility and reality of sharing faith – that is, evangelising – diminishes or ceases within a family or community, or when approaches in doing so become ineffective, Christian faith degenerates and may even die.

Jesus highlighted for his followers their central part in leading others to him. He directed them, as recorded in Mark's Gospel, to 'go into all the whole world and proclaim the good news to the whole creation' (Mk 16:15). These words are all the more striking when we consider that they were his final direction to and wish for his disciples. Here, he relayed his final testament immediately before he was 'taken up to heaven'. Without delay, his followers seem to have set about the task of proclamation: 'and they went out and proclaimed the good news everywhere, while the Lord worked with them and confirmed the message by the signs that accompanied it' (Mk 16:20).

Matthew records a similar scenario: 'Go, therefore, make disciples of all nations' (Mt 28:19). He too presents the final wish and words of Jesus as a clear command to his followers to 'make disciples'. They were to go in his name and point all whom they met towards him, and to know him as their guide, wisdom and teacher. It is interesting to note that Jesus was not speaking here to self-confident, assured and well-trained followers. Rather, as Matthew records, 'some doubted' who he was as he stood before them (Mt 28:17). His words must have appeared extremely idealistic and strange to them. Perhaps Matthew was observing that they were challenged to the point of helplessness, and carried a deep need for his assurance. This may explain his inclusion of the Lord's pledge: 'I am with you always, to the end of the age' (Mt 28:20).

Second Vatican Council

The Second Vatican Council gave momentum to understanding evangelisation as a central component in the life of every Christian believer and community. In doing so, it addressed what had become the almost exclusive linking of mission with geographical expansion, which had involved sending religious professionals to places where Christ was not known. The primary purpose for evangelisation had been new conversions in foreign territories.

The council did include this 'work of the missions', but equally emphasised that the entire Church 'is by its very nature missionary' because 'it has its origin in the mission of the Son and the Holy Spirit'.[7] Evangelisation is thus no longer limited to territory but is lived wherever Christian believers share faith with other people.

The council moves from an emphasis on geography to people, and understands that evangelisation is within the obligation and capacity of all believers. It stresses that every baptised person is called to mission. To be baptised is to be called and sent to live and witness to one's Christian faith. The council explains that the Spirit of Christ continues his activity and inspires 'in the hearts of the faithful that same spirit of mission which impelled Christ himself'.[8] This *missio Dei*, this being sent in the Spirit, is intended to 'lead other people to faith, freedom and peace in Christ … and … to open up for all people a free and sure path to full participation in the mystery of Christ'.[9]

All Christian believers are called to bear witness to Christ in their local situations through their network of relationships 'in the family, in their social group, and in the sphere of their profession'.[10] This network affords them 'countless opportunities for exercising the apostolate of evangelisation and sanctification'.[11] They do this initially through their wordless example. However, the council goes on to

7   *AGD*, 2.
8   Ibid., 4.
9   Ibid., 5.
10 Ibid., 21.
11 AA, 6.

say that there is also a time for words to explain the basis of one's faith and hope: 'The true apostle is on the lookout for occasions of announcing Christ by word, either to unbelievers to draw them towards the faith, or to the faithful to instruct them, strengthen them, incite them to a more fervent life, "for Christ's love urges us on" (2 Cor 5:14).'[12] It is for this reason that the council stresses the importance of lay formation, because many people will not hear the Gospel and come to acknowledge Christ except through the lay people with whom they associate.[13]

In the intervening years, there has been much reflection on evangelisation as the 'special grace and vocation of the Church', and as her 'essential function'.[14] As 'essential', it cannot be ignored, delayed or set aside, without betraying the nature of the Church. For this reason, too, every Christian believer must engage in the task of evangelising. Not to do so is to live faith in a diminished, inward-looking and incomplete way. It amounts to a certain denial of what it means to be a Christian disciple. Faith, properly understood, propels us towards another to alleviate suffering and share our hope in Christ who dispels our inner emptiness and loneliness. When this is lacking, an essential ingredient in Christian living is missing.

Evangelisation is no easy task. It is not straightforward and uniform. Rather, it takes many forms, for example silent witness, proclaiming the basic elements of the life, death and resurrection of Jesus (*kerygma*), catechesis of children, adult formation, engaging in issues of justice and world peace, celebration of sacraments, and life within Christian community. As such, it may be difficult to define and to describe. It easily runs the risk of meaning nothing in practice when it embraces so much, and hence may lose the ability to motivate people towards action.

12   Ibid.
13   Ibid., 13.
14   *EN*, 20. For Pope Paul VI, a central question is how people of faith might dialogue with cultures that have lost or are losing elements of their Christian roots in a way that is respectful of their local stories and traditions. This, for him, is an urgent dialogue because of the great rift that is taking place between 'the Gospel and culture'.

Saint John Paul II

For Pope Paul IV, 'there is no true evangelisation if the name, the teaching, the life, the promises, the kingdom and the mystery of Jesus of Nazareth, the Son of God, are not proclaimed'.[15] Neither does it occur without the influence of the Holy Spirit because it is much more than a good idea, detailed analysis, skills in communication, or a clear plan: 'Techniques of evangelisation are valuable, but even though they be perfect they cannot dispense with the secret action of the Holy Spirit'.[16]

In 1983, Saint John Paul II outlined that evangelisation is to be characterised by newness in 'ardour, methods and expression'.[17] Each of these words carries rich significance for him. 'Ardour' refers to personal enthusiasm and arises from the radical newness of knowing Christ. 'Method' indicates that evangelisation is to involve all Christian believers. 'Expression' suggests the creativity that emerges from personal faith in Christ as people seek to engage in the work of justice and speak his word.

During the following years, John Paul II continued to hone what he saw as the relevance of new evangelisation, especially in the Western world. In 1990, for example, he declared his sense that the moment had come for the Church to commit all its 'energies to a new evangelisation' as its 'supreme duty'.[18] He had come to recognise that 'entire groups of the baptised have lost a living sense of the faith, or even no longer consider themselves members of the Church, and live a life far removed from Christ (and his Gospel)' … and that … 'in this case what is needed is a "new evangelisation"',[19] which called for radically new approaches.

New evangelisation must not be left to 'specialists',[20] but must involve all the members of the People of God. It must set a new

15   *EN*, 22.
16   Ibid., 75.
17   Pope John Paul II, Port-au-Prince, Haiti (9 March 1983).
18   *RM*, 3.
19   Ibid., 33.
20   *CL*, 40.

priority for the Church. This means that we, as Christian believers, must 'revive in ourselves the burning conviction of Paul, who cried out, "Woe to me if I do not preach the Gospel" (1 Cor 9:16)'.[21] It implies the formation and nourishment of people who, with passion, will stir a new mission and 'apostolic outreach, and 'live the everyday commitment of Christian communities and groups'.[22] The principle at work here is very simple: 'Those who have come into genuine contact with Christ cannot keep him for themselves; they must proclaim him.'[23]

Benedict XVI also gave much time to evangelisation in his addresses and writings. For him, the Holy Spirit is always at work in the life of believers and the Church, as their source of faith and joy. In fact, 'the Holy Spirit is joy',[24] and the reason for evangelisation. For Benedict XVI, 'to evangelise is to seek to communicate the joy of the Holy Spirit',[25] who guides Christian believers to find new ways beyond complex situations to effectively communicate the word of God.

The relevance and urgency of evangelisation is that it seeks what is best for individuals and society. It intends the renewal and advance of every individual and of the entire human race, together with the environment that surrounds them.[26] As such, it is love in action. It leads people to authentic freedom and fulfilment, and to recognising their source in Christ, who has restored them to their dignity and given meaning to life.[27] In these terms then, evangelisation expresses the greatest act of loving and serving that a Christian believer can render another person and all humanity. Conversely, not to evangelise is to withhold one's love from another.

---

21 Ibid.
22 Ibid.
23 Ibid.
24 Benedict XVI, Christmas Address to the Roman Curia, 2008.
25 Ibid.
26 *EN*, 18.
27 *RM*, 2.

Focus

In conclusion, evangelisation calls for the active involvement of all who are baptised. It is part of the Church's essential nature. As 'essential', it is a defining and identifying feature of what it means to be a 'Church' person. In other words, it is clear that each person, each community, association, institution, parish and diocese, to be called Christian, is to evangelise.

I note that this sense of urgency demands the conversion and renewal of all the baptised in a way that leads to their active involvement in evangelisation that is new. This implies in particular formation that will lead them to witness to their faith within all the spheres of their activity and influence, and in this way be a Christian presence and voice at the frontiers of contemporary culture.

Formation, in this sense, can never be equated with information, techniques and tactics. New evangelisation can never be undertaken as a human endeavour alone nor as a good and noble idea with well-worked-out planning. No, it is inextricably linked with Pentecost. Without a new Pentecost there is no new evangelisation. In other words, evangelisation that is new bears fruit only when the Spirit of God inspires individuals and communities with great creativity, zeal, courage and wisdom to undertake new paths. John Paul II says that 'we must rekindle in ourselves the impetus of the beginnings and allow ourselves to be filled with the ardour of the apostolic preaching which followed Pentecost'.[28] Evangelisation, then, must always be accompanied with sincere prayer for a new advent of the Holy Spirit – a new Pentecost, as at the Church's beginnings.

There appears to be a long road ahead. Much evidence suggests that direct evangelisation is undertaken by a very small percentage of the Catholic population. Indeed, for many believers, it seems to evoke elements of fear and suspicion, and, at best, uncertainty as to what it might entail.

For Pope Francis the Church has lost much of its 'evangelical

28   *NMI*, 40.

fervour'.[29] For this reason it becomes stagnant and sick, and gives rise to pettiness, inward-looking attitudes and empty rituals among Christian people. For him, this 'can only be healed by breathing in the pure air of the Holy Spirit who frees us from self-centredness cloaked in an outward religiosity bereft of God'.[30] His appeal leaves us with no room for ambiguity: 'Let us not allow ourselves to be robbed of the Gospel!'[31] but journey towards the freedom of knowing Christ.

Inspiring Faith Communities is a programme of evangelisation. It intends to initiate, or support, a process of evangelisation that is new in 'ardour, method and expression'. It calls people to discipleship. In doing so, it points them to conversion and to friendship with Christ. In the hands of people who are already awakened to the gift of God's Spirit, this programme is a powerful tool and facilitates freedom and the conviction of the dynamic presence and influence of the Holy Spirit.

29   *EG*, 95.
30   Ibid., 97.
31   Ibid., 97.

Chapter 4

Renewal of Parish ~ Pope Francis

'IN ALL its activities the parish encourages and trains its members to be evangelisers. It is a community of communities, a sanctuary where the thirsty come to drink in the midst of their journey, and a centre of constant missionary outreach.'[32]

In this chapter, I reflect upon my third conviction that inspires and gives direction to *Inspiring Faith Communities*, namely, the importance of parish in the renewal of God's people. I do so largely through the lens of *Evangelii Gaudium*, where Pope Francis provides us with pastoral sightlines and parameters in the task of parish renewal, and displays remarkable ability to prompt us to reimagine new pastoral emphases and approaches. I conclude that for him missionary discipleship is to be a distinguishing feature of every parish, which in turn calls for a new pastoral conversion.

Missionary Discipleship

Pope Francis uses the phrase, 'missionary discipleship' nine times in the *Evangelii Gaudium*. In this way, he points towards the ideal of parish life where every believer is at the same time a disciple and a missionary. For him 'every Christian is a missionary to the extent that he or she has encountered the love of God in Christ Jesus.'[33]

He thus sees that the parish has a twofold task. It seeks to accompany parishioners to encounter and to engage ever more trustingly with

32   Ibid., 28.
33   Ibid., 120.

the person of Christ. Equally, it seeks to empower them to move with missionary conviction and faith towards all people. Being a disciple and a missionary are inherently linked together when there is maturity of faith for an individual or parish. The contemplative journey, undertaken inwards towards the intimacy of divine love, and the missionary journey outwards towards all, at the same time nourish, complement and fulfil each other.

In employing the term 'missionary discipleship', Pope Francis proposes a new departure and a new path for every parishioner and parish. He calls for a spiritual conversion as yielding to the call of Jesus to be his disciples, who know the freedom he gives. He equally calls for a pastoral and missionary conversion that invites all parishioners to be 'permanently in a state of mission'.[34] They are to see themselves, and what they do, through the radar of 'evangelical discernment'.[35] Their criterion of evaluation becomes the degree to which a parish and its parishioners evangelise and contribute to the transformation of people and society. They are to evaluate current parish and Church structures according to whether they help or hamper evangelisation, while discerning new structures that will contribute to new missionary outreaches. For Pope Francis, newness in parish evangelisation clearly necessitates an ecclesial conversion.

Pope Francis describes the parish, with images that clearly communicate its place in society. Parish is, for him, a sanctuary, which satiates people's thirst, and which is 'first and foremost a people advancing on its pilgrim way towards God'.[36] Through such images, Pope Francis places people rather than institution and structures to the fore in thinking about parish. In this way, he draws attention to the parish as a people who are searching and responding to the invitation of the Lord, and who help one another as fellow pilgrims. This involves being sensitive to all who are searching and seeking a place of understanding and healing, and during times of suffering

34   Ibid., 25.
35   Ibid., 50.
36   Ibid., 111.

and struggle, to 'hear the cry for justice and to respond to it with all their might'.[37]

Disciples who know the transforming love of Jesus become open to the influence and gifts of his Spirit and, in the words of Pope Francis, they cease to 'cage the Spirit of God'. This experience teaches them to expect to be surprised and to know the presence, love and guiding wisdom of God's Spirit as living and daily realities. It also teaches them to reach out to others with love, expectant like the first disciples. As they went forth, 'the Lord worked with them and confirmed the message'.[38]

For Pope Francis, enthusiasm for mission arises when a person knows that Jesus 'walks with him, speaks to him, breathes with him, and works with him.'[39] On the other hand, conviction for evangelisation wanes when people no longer 'savour' Christ's friendship and his love. To 'savour' in this way involves giving a priority of time in 'standing before him with open hearts, letting him look at us',[40] and having the support of a community of disciples.

At the core of discipleship and evangelisation is the Spirit of God, and what Pope Francis calls 'the grace of baptism in the Holy Spirit'.[41] He understands this as a mysterious intervention of the Holy Spirit. It leads to a conversion of life. It makes pastoral action fruitful. The individual recognises the intervention of God as grace, while praise of God, prayer, scripture and the sacraments take on new significance. At the same time, it commits one to share this grace of baptism in the Holy Spirit with all people through evangelisation, spiritual ecumenism, care of the poor and needy and hospitality for the marginalised. Mission then, for Pope Francis, is both 'a passion for Jesus and a passion for his people'.[42]

---

37 Ibid., 188.
38 Ibid., 275.
39 Ibid., 266.
40 Ibid., 264.
41 Pope Francis, Address to the Catholic Charismatic Renewal, (Olympic stadium, Rome, 1 June 2014).
42 *EG*, 268.

Discipleship with Respect

Discipleship has its roots in 'savouring the friendship of Jesus, and his message'.[43] This can never remain simply a personal comfort. That would distort its purpose and limit it to an inward-looking exercise. Rather, it must inspire people to look beyond themselves and evangelise. Pope Francis asks, 'What kind of love would not feel the need to speak of the beloved, to point him out, to make him known?'[44] True discipleship, for him, is to be missionary, and to be 'constantly ready to bring the love of Jesus to others'.[45] When a person experiences true friendship with Jesus she or he also knows the difference he makes, and will be eager to tell others how he enriches life and brings meaning.

Pope Francis draws attention to how we can best approach our daily conversations. For him, the first step is to have total respect for the person and freedom of the other,[46] and 'accept and esteem others as companions along the way ... learning to find Jesus in the faces of others'.[47] This involves dialogue and deep listening, which gives others the freedom and opportunity to talk about their joys and disappointments, hopes and concerns.

Then, once trust and friendship have been established, Pope Francis recommends that we share something of the word of God as an expression of our love. This can be a verse or a story from scripture, with reference to the personal love of God. He sees that humility before God and before the other person is fundamental in that we are fellow pilgrims. More especially, 'the message is so rich and so deep that it always exceeds our grasp'.[48] I find this a lovely phrase as it suggests that we will only ever understand God in a limited way. Yet, at the same time, we can expect God to use our efforts to have an influence far greater than we intend or imagine. Pope Francis suggests that there are times when, after people have engaged in conversations

43   Ibid., 266.
44   Ibid., 264.
45   Ibid., 127.
46   Ibid., 128.
47   Ibid., 91.
48   Ibid., 128.

of a personal nature, it is appropriate to end with a prayer together. In this way, he says, people will know that they have been listened to, that God is interested in their situation, and that he is close to them and speaks to them.

Encounter

The idea of 'closeness' is a recurring theme in the addresses and writings of Pope Francis. Every Christian believer and every institution, whether Church, diocese or parish, is to be close to people. This is the mark of faith, and indicates true loving. Thus, Pope Francis exhorts pastors and shepherds to have the 'smell of the sheep', and calls every evangeliser to 'develop a spiritual taste for being close to people's lives'.[49] In other words, everyone who evangelises is to walk among people, listening to them and hearing their stories.

Pope Francis seeks a Church that is poor and for the poor. He wants a Church to take on an option for the poor and put them 'at the centre of the Church's pilgrim way'.[50] Commitment to the poor is not to consist exclusively in activities and programmes. More fundamentally, it is about becoming their friends. It is to listen to them, hear their experiences of life and of their culture, respect them as persons, touch their beauty beyond their appearances and seek what is best for them. In this way they will be our teachers. For the poor, it will be their path towards freedom. It is only when real and sincere closeness exists that 'the poor feel at home'.[51] For Pope Francis, every Christian believer is to find ways that lead the poor towards maturity in faith because he observes that 'the worst discrimination which the poor suffer is the lack of spiritual care', and that a preferential option for the poor 'must translate into a privileged and preferential religious care'.[52] This will involve entering into relationships and closeness with them so that they experience acceptance and community, and are accompanied step by step in becoming missionary disciples.

49 Ibid., 268.
50 Ibid., 198.
51 Ibid., 199.
52 Ibid., 200.

'A field hospital after battle' is a most compelling image that Pope Francis uses in describing the Church.[53] In this way, he draws attention to the necessity to be close to and among people who are deeply hurting. He outlines that 'to heal wounds, and to warm the hearts of the faithful; it (the Church) needs nearness, proximity'.[54] Hurting arises from material, financial or educational poverty, or from social exclusion. For him, 'the ministers of the Gospel (and evangelists) must be people who can warm the hearts of the people, who walk through the dark night with them, who know how to dialogue and to descend themselves into their people's night, into the darkness, but without getting lost'.[55] The Church must thus find 'new roads to step outside itself' in its service of all who are hurting.[56]

For Pope Francis, the word 'encounter' is charged with meaning. Faith, for him, 'is an encounter with Jesus'.[57] From this he urges that 'we must do the same as Jesus did, and meet others as they are. We must bring about encounter. We are to make our faith a culture of encounter and of friendship, a culture wherein we find brothers and sisters, when we can talk even with those who do not think like us, even with those who have a different faith.'[58]

The parish, as community of disciples, witnesses to a new way of being together in the world. It announces a world where peoples and nations can live at peace with one another. It acts as 'a radiant and attractive witness of fraternal communion'.[59] It exists to bring life and peace to people, proclaim the good news and bring healing. It must therefore avoid presenting religion as placing burdens upon people and as 'a form of servitude, whereas God's mercy has willed that we should be free'.[60]

A New Evangelisation

53 Antonio Spadaro, editor-in-chief of the Italian Jesuit journal, *La Civiltà Cattolica*, 20 September 2013, where he quotes his interview with Pope Francis.
54 Ibid.
55 Ibid.
56 Ibid. According to Pope Francis, this also corresponds with the wishes of the people of God want who 'pastors, not clergy acting like bureaucrats or government officials'.
57 Pope Francis, address during Pentecost vigil in St Peter's, 18 May 2013.
58 Ibid.
59 *EG*, 99.
60 Ibid., 43.

In *Evangelii Gaudium* Pope Francis emphasises features of newness in the evangelisation of parish. He explicitly outlines his vision of parish life as 'an environment for hearing God's word'.[61] Parish thus exists as a service to people, which facilitates them in hearing the word of God, and in deepening and celebrating their relationship with Christ. This vision sets the spirit of worship, renewal, proclamation and outreach for a parish community.

For Pope Francis, the parish is to ensure that 'in all its activities it [parish] encourages and trains its members to be evangelisers' and remain 'completely mission oriented'.[62] A parish community does not set limits about whom it will embrace and welcome. Rather, it reaches out to all people as it offers a 'sanctuary where the thirsty come to drink in the midst of their journey, and a centre of constant missionary outreach'.[63]

There are times when I detect impatience in Pope Francis. He urges people to evangelise, go, reach out, do it. They have so much to give, he claims, and yet they remain silent and keep the message 'caged'. I find a good example of this when he advises that every Christian who knows God's personal love does not need much training. He urges people 'to go out and proclaim that love'.[64] Every Christian has a personal story of faith to share. He explains, 'In your heart you know that is not the same to live without him; when you have come to realise, what has helped you to live and given you hope, is what you also need to communicate to others. Our falling short of perfection should be no excuse.'[65]

Pope Francis observes that for parish renewal a Spirit-filled evangelisation is necessary today.[66] He thus invites every parishioner to give the Holy Spirit permission to be a guide and to expect to be led to adopt new attitudes and new approaches. This means

61 Ibid., 28.
62 Ibid.
63 Ibid.
64 Ibid., 120.
65 Ibid., 121.
66 Ibid, 259–61. Pope Francis in these paragraphs refers to all Christian believers, and thus is inclusive of every parishioner.

renouncing the attempt to plan and control everything, while being open to the guidance of the Holy Spirit, who enlightens, guides and directs us, and who knows what is needed in every time and place. 'This is what it means to be mysteriously fruitful.'[67] Such openness, he sees, inspires a missionary impulse that intends, and is capable of, transforming everything, including individuals and society. It calls the parish, for example, to examine and redirect its customs, ways of doing things, times and schedules, language and structures in a such way that it will lead to 'the evangelisation of today's world, rather than her self-preservation'.[68]

The Art of Accompaniment

Pope Francis places great emphasis on what he calls the 'art of accompaniment' in a new method of living one's Christian faith. He recognises that Christian living matures only gradually. Indeed, it takes a lifetime to grow into what it means that God is present in the saving work of Jesus Christ through his life, death and resurrection, and into its implications for one's life. He claims that we will not achieve this on our own. We need an individual or a community to support us. We need, he claims, a 'compassionate gaze, which heals, liberates and encourages growth in the Christian life'.[69] In other words, we need a human touch, which completes growth that is personal, gradual and according to God's wisdom. He calls this process and dynamic 'the art of accompaniment'. It is so important for him that he invites everyone, clergy, religious and laity, to live this process, both in accompanying others, and in being accompanied.

At the core of the art of accompaniment is humility, honesty and openness before another person. It means attentive listening to another. It 'teaches us to remove our sandals before the sacred ground of the other'. Its intention is our spiritual maturing and how we are discerning the vision of God for ourselves in the midst of our

67   Ibid., 280.
68   Ibid., 27.
69   Ibid., 169.

relationships and activities, which may at times impinge upon us as very complex. Its intention, too, is to lead to the flourishing of faith as service through work for justice and evangelisation.[70]

The 'art of accompaniment' is also important because we can never fully grasp the person of Jesus and his message at any one time. At best we only gradually appropriate it. We remain forever pilgrims. Hence, Pope Francis calls for 'a pedagogy which will introduce people step by step'[71] to know the mystery of God and life as missionary disciples.

Hope

My hope is that *Inspiring Faith Communities* will contribute, however little, to parish renewal and evangelisation. More fundamentally, I hope that it will make available a step-by-step process to accompany parishioners in knowing the freedom that friendship with Jesus the Lord gives, in discerning the structures that will support them as disciples and as missionaries, and in reaching out beyond themselves with merciful love.

I have outlined the convictions that have inspired *Inspiring Faith Communities*. My reason for doing so is to prompt every reader to reflect upon her or his own local situation, and to invite to the surface their ambitions and wishes for their parish. I also hope that catching a glimpse of the motivations that underpin the programme will be of interest to those who host it; that it will expand the possibilities they see in hosting it, and prepare them for the expected harvest. The next chapter will outline some practical help in the preparation and planning of the programme.

Chapter 5

70 Ibid., 172. The art of accompaniment is thus to be distinguished from therapy, which 'supports self-absorption and ceases to be a pilgrimage with Christ to the Father' (*EG*, 170).
71 Ibid., 171.

Planning

ON THE basis of what I have seen and heard, I am convinced that *Inspiring Faith Communities* works. However, it does not do so automatically. There is no escape from good planning and preparation. As someone said, to fail to prepare is to prepare to fail. For me, a number of elements need to fit together as a programme of preparation. The first concerns knowing what you wish to achieve. Hence, it is important to reflect on your reason(s) for undertaking this programme. While you may not have this fully and clearly worked out, you will need to have at least some sense of why you wish to host it, and what you wish to see happen.

For me, *Inspiring Faith Communities* works best as an effort of evangelisation. It leads people towards becoming disciples who know new life and freedom in Christ, while at the same time it encourages those whom they meet to discipleship.

I used this programme initially in the parish of St John's the Evangelist, Ballinteer, Dublin, to reach out to people who did not see themselves as very involved in their faith and to lead them to a deeper decision for Christ. I put it together in response to quite a struggle that was going on for me at a personal level as I observed a growing gap between spirituality and life. I observed that what people professed in church on Sunday seemed to have little impact upon what they did on Monday.

A central element in preparing to host this programme is not only familiarity with the programme itself but, most importantly, the preparation of the heart. By this I mean that the programme works best when it is rooted in prayer. You, and those who are centrally involved in its preparation, need to commit to a daily time of personal prayer. Prayer needs be a feature of each planning meeting. You might also consider investing the prayer of other people, for example, fellow parishioners, or those in religious communities. My experience tells me that planning may appear daunting, but when people are praying the various tasks fall easily into place and obstacles have a way of evaporating or opening up other opportunities.

Pray about what you wish to do, and especially about God's plan. This programme intends to lead people to a new or deeper encounter with Christ and the experience of a community. As such, preparation must have its roots in prayer, the word of God and openness to God's plan. It is necessary to prepare our hearts and not just the practicalities of the programme. What happens in the private spaces of our lives determines our influence in the public spaces. What happens beneath the surface in our hearts determines the impact of the programme upon individuals and community. Hence, 'pray, pray, pray', as individuals, and with others during the various phases of the programme. Also, consider a prayer campaign and invest the prayer of, for example, religious communities, parishioners and friends.

This chapter offers you a step-by-step approach to planning *Inspiring Faith Communities* in a way that will lead participants to a renewal of faith, and contribute to parish evangelisation. It presents some simple guidelines and suggestions to help make it a successful event for you. You will, of course, need to adapt what you read here to suit your own circumstances.

When Is the Best Time to Run the Programme?
The programme can begin at any time. The two issues here are: a) length of preparation time for a launch. It is wise to think in terms of months as you gather a guiding team, advertise and decide on the various tasks to be undertaken; b) the best time for a launch – Lent, September and autumn (including Advent) seem to be times when

people are especially open to undertaking something new.

Where?

Wherever you can create conversation, reflection and freedom from distractions. Hence, it may be hosted anywhere, such as a private room, community centre, parish hall, church, any public amenity or someone's home.

For How Many?

This programme is adaptable and can take place with a small number of friends, neighbours or colleagues, or with a large gathering.

For Whom?

Anyone, young or old, who wishes to experience a more personal and living faith will benefit greatly.

Clear Reason

Verbalising your reason for hosting this programme is one of the most important steps. It may be helpful to write it down. In this way it will become clearer to you and will also serve to guide you throughout your preparation. It is not sufficient that it be simply 'putting on' another activity, or 'taking up' what appears to be a good idea. Its purpose, I believe, needs to run deeper. If, for example, you wish to initiate a process to help people share their faith with others, or to explore their faith as it relates to everyday events and relationships, here you have a resource that will be of great benefit to you. If you genuinely believe that small faith communities can be places of formation and community, you have here an ideal opportunity to begin working towards them. Through this programme, you facilitate for others a more living faith and a network of relationships. In this way, you lay a foundation for faith communities, which will nourish all who participate and prepare them to go forth to evangelise. For whom do you intend this programme? This is a related question. Your answer here will determine your advertising strategy and the emphasis of the programme.

Time and Location

You now decide where and when the course may take place. You may already have agreed on your preferred location, and even determined its availability. In the event of wishing to host the course as a parish event, you will need to share your thinking and hopes with the parish team, and/or with others in key pastoral positions within the parish. This may also serve as an opportune moment to invest the help and support you might need. The important feature here is to communicate clearly what you plan.

Guiding Team

It is important at an early stage of preparation to involve other people with whom you share your hopes as well as the various tasks that arise. A few meetings together may be sufficient.

Selection of Speakers

Speakers have greatest impact when they address their theme and speak out of their personal friendship with Christ and commitment to evangelisation. Hence, inputs from people who live the communitarian and ecclesial dimensions of faith, for example parish cell participants, can greatly contribute to the programme and bring it to life. This applies in particular to the final presentation. It is also important to give each speaker a clear and specific brief, with expected speaking time, and a copy of *Inspiring Faith Communities* for their personal help and information.

I have observed that nominating a person who speaks at the beginning of each meeting contributes greatly to continuity. His or her tasks are to welcome participants publicly, introduce the theme for each night, briefly share a personal faith story, which is related to the previous week or the theme for the current one, put people at ease and call forward the person who is to proclaim the scripture. This may take no more than three minutes. This person may also act as coordinator for the duration of the programme. I also highly recommend a time-keeper for the duration of the programme.

Music Requirement

The area of music calls for careful discernment. On one occasion I witnessed *Inspiring Faith Communities* with no music except during the fifth meeting. During a subsequent programme we had music of a joy-filled nature. We learned that while music and singing did set an atmosphere of welcome and community participation, it seemed to make little difference in terms of the impact upon individuals in the different programmes. It is thus best to make decisions while observing the background, age and number of participants. Selected hymns and music need to be simple and of high quality, encouraging the participation of all in praise of God, with words available to all.

Finances

Covering the cost of the programme can be a vexed issue. I have seen four different methods of meeting costs. One – the parish covers all costs; two – participants make contributions and parish pays the deficit; three – participants make contributions while the deficit is covered by those who run the programme; four – a benefactor covers the cost. I tend towards participants having the option of making a contribution.

Advertising

Key questions here include, who are the target audience(s)? Who do you wish to attract? What do you expect to emerge from the programme? The answers will have an impact on shaping your advertising strategy.

Advertising is a crucial area. You simply do not need a well-run event that few people know about. A creative approach to advertising is therefore essential. Surveys suggest that people more often attend such events because another person invited them, so you need a good system of encouraging all involved to invite family members, friends and work and leisure colleagues. Develop a system of sending emails and letters of promotion and invitation to as wide a circle of people as possible. Draw upon those creative individuals who are part of every community to advertise the programme, and especially through social media, for example Facebook, Instagram and Twitter.

It is important to use the usual channels of church notices, posters for porches and public places, local radio and newspapers. Many religious magazines and papers usually welcome material, particularly when it is cast in story form. A two-minute presentation made during Sunday masses one to two weeks before the event is very effective. Large billboards in public spaces attract a lot of attention. I know of one area where people distributed flyers at the local shopping mall and spoke with those who passed by. Each group needs to draw up its own plans and time frame.

Ambience

A space communicates. We often think simply of a place of meeting, without reference to its language. It is thus important to think of its ambience with creativity and arrange for suitable lighting, colour, banner(s), podium, table with cloth, bible and candle, flowers, flipchart, gentle music as people enter, and a room that is not uncomfortably hot or cold.[72] It is also important to give much thought to the seating arrangement. I tend to move away from the 'classroom effect' of straight rows with the speaker(s) to the front, preferring seating of six to ten chairs being previously arranged in semi-circles. The hosts welcome people as they arrive and usher them towards available seats. This ensures an informal seating arrangement. It also enables the speaker to be towards the front but in a way that she or he is noticeably part of the gathered community.

---

72   It may also help to have the facility to project a presentation or words of hymns on to a screen.

A desk is placed beforehand beside the entrance to the meeting place. On arrival, participants are given a name tag with their Christian name and a copy of the accompanying booklet, *Living Word*, on which is written a particular number. Meanwhile, those whose task it is to staff the desk write down, on entry, the names and numbers. There may be certain advantages in assigning the same number to friends as this indicates the group in which people will later participate. Follow-up may be easier when friends have shared the same experience. However, this should be left to the judgement of those organising the programme.

Small Group Host
When I mention 'small group', I have in mind a cluster of six to ten people, including a host(s) who facilitates their discussions. Such a group is large enough to ensure a good range and exchange of experiences, while sufficiently small to encourage the participation of all. People are placed in such groupings to have a good conversation in response to the presentations and stories they have already heard. Towards the end of the programme participants are likely to comment on how attractive and helpful they found these small groups, even though they may have been somewhat apprehensive during the first meeting or two. My own explanation is that people love having a place where they can freely express their opinions and raise questions; where a high degree of confidentiality exists; and where they know they will not be judged. It is perhaps also likely that they will realise how much and how deeply they believe, as they put their faith into words, or at least seek to verbalise it. This seems to be particularly true of our present times when many people perceive that everything has changed, including even the basics of the Christian faith.

A small group can organise and direct its own conversations. However, the presence of someone, previously nominated, who holds the vision and direction of the group, greatly benefits the individuals involved and the quality of harmony and participation. It simplifies the dynamics that normally arise when a group is forming and norming. It establishes order within the group. All are aware of the person who has overall responsibility. This removes from participants the responsibility of initiating discussion and giving it direction, so that they can enjoy and benefit from the experience. It takes away the uncertainty of 'what happens next?'

What are we to call such a 'holder'? I suggest either facilitator or host. The value of each of these titles is that they place emphasis on their role as service to the group gathered, and away from being experts or leaders who take participants to a determined destination. The advantage of 'facilitator' is that it implies the importance of each person's input and participation, while that of 'host' is that it highlights a welcome to each person and their contribution to the quality of the group. You may have another preferred name. For simplicity, and not to imply preference, I use 'host' throughout this book, when I refer to this role.

The primary contribution of hosts is that they model Christian living for participants. In other words, they are seen to be making a genuine effort to live and grow in their faith. They know the difference that Christ makes for them. They know they have greater peace, hope, meaning and sense of personal well-being in and through him. They are his disciples who are eager to follow him and learn about his call upon their lives. Their impulse is to invite others to discipleship and to understanding God's call and mission for them in contemporary culture. For this reason, their lives mirror what it means to be a missionary disciple beyond what they say, and 'speak' beyond their expectations. At the same time, they are aware they will not have answers to questions they may be asked. This does not perturb them as they live with a deep confidence that the Holy Spirit gives them wisdom and words as needed.[73]

Hosts make every effort to be good listeners, who respect and welcome people with their different viewpoints and perspectives. They resist the temptation to give the 'correct' answer and, more

73   John 14:26.

crucially, to correct another on some aspect of his or her personal faith or practice. Their relationship with participants is not that of teacher and pupils. Rather they genuinely welcome each person's contribution, even though it may be at variance with some of their own beliefs and practices. They are fellow pilgrims who gather in a common quest for freedom, peace and truth.

The really important role for the host is to help keep the focus on personal responses. There is a great temptation, on the part of many people, to speak about what they think about issues, rather than what they feel about their personal realities. This can be a way of distancing themselves, albeit unconsciously, from what is personal. It calls for a delicacy of approach on the part of the host, as many people may be in such an environment for the first time, and it may take two or three meetings before they feel at home. This may be further complicated in that going off on tangents can, at times, seem very attractive to all, including the host. It is thus most important that the host is alert to what is happening, and encourages contributions of a personal nature.

A heart that loves and seeks what is best for each individual motivates the hosts. At the same time, they may initially be extremely fearful at the prospect of hosting a group. Hosts will not take themselves too seriously, as they are deeply convinced that they will not make faith happen in another, that only God's Spirit can do this. They are happy simply to be available and facilitate conversion and the action of the Holy Spirit.

It is preferable to have two hosts for each small group. This diminishes the sense of responsibility for people who may never have acted in such a capacity. It enables one person to take a lead role for a particular meeting, or for part of it, and roles can be reversed when the groups next meet. It means that the review of the meeting becomes a good learning event for both hosts, as each shares observations, strengths and weaknesses about what has happened, about the quality of their own participation, and makes suggestions for future meetings. Co-hosting a small group also establishes a degree of community in the group from the beginning.

What to Look for in a Host?

Missionary discipleship should be evident, at least to some extent, in those whom we identify as hosts. This includes evidence of integrity in the way they live, and of a genuine effort to be in right relationships with their family, neighbours, and work and leisure colleagues. It is not about seeking those who are perfect, but rather those who seek to do the best they can in life and who know their need of God. Pope Francis and Rabbi Abraham Skorka brought this point into focus when they wrote, 'the great leaders of God's people were men who left room for doubt … One of the characteristics of a bad leader is to be excessively normative because of his self-assurance … When someone is self-sufficient, when he has all the answers to every question, it is proof that God is not with him.'[74]

Possible hosts display an ability to work with other people, and draw out the best in them. They show flexibility, openness and an encouraging attitude in their relationships. These traits are important because a central focus of the host is to draw participants into a process of self-discovery and renewal. The emphasis of selection, then, is to find hosts who will facilitate participants in the articulation of their insights, hopes, questions and frustrations and, in this way, become pilgrims together (with one another and with the host) as they journey towards God. This is a key point, in that the members of each group, including hosts, learn to become active participants and pilgrims together, in the process of renewal and self-discovery.

Where to Look for Hosts

The selection of hosts is most important as you prepare to run your first *Inspiring Faith Communities*. Now that you know the qualities you are seeking, your next question is where you will find such hosts. My simple answer is to pray about possibilities, talk about what you

---

74 Jorge Mario Bergoglio and Abraham Skorka, *On Heaven and Earth*, London: Bloomsbury, 2013; Spanish original, 2010.

plan to do, observe people who worship with the parish, enquire about who may have already run somewhat similar programmes, and recognise people who genuinely seek a richer spirituality. I have at times seen that the quiet, seeming silent churchgoer who is not publicly involved in ministry or activity is a great untapped source. The ideal is pitched above, now do what is possible in your unique situation. Walk in faith. What I have observed convinces me that when a person commits to what seems to be the Lord's work, he prompts people and sends fellow pilgrims to bring a particular task to completion.

The initial hosting of this programme will identify a number of participants with the qualities to be good hosts. A mixture of people who are new and experienced as hosts works very well.

In hosting an initial *Inspiring Faith Communities*, I know parishes that have adopted different approaches. A number have invited one or more people who have already hosted this programme in another parish to journey with them through the various stages of preparation, hosting and follow-up. Others have delegated a team of people from a neighbouring parish to run this programme on their behalf. I also know of examples where a small group of five to ten people have undertaken the programme together in order to experience it and learn about making it available to all parishioners at a later date.

How to Select a Host
You may already have spoken to people with a view to their acting as hosts. At the same time, I think it best to issue each individual with a written invitation. In this way you can communicate a sense of mission in a personal way, and you have the possibility of outlining what is expected of hosts in terms of their input and time commitment, together with the purpose, content, duration and times of the programme.

This invitation, even when it is somewhat expected, generally brings to the surface issues for the recipients, such as their hopes, fears and sense of unworthiness. Their response will provide an opportunity for you to explore with them the meaning of Christian service and discipleship, while assessing their suitability as hosts. It is always important that the final decision rests with the invited persons. This provides them the space to discern whether or not they are called, at this time, to the tasks as outlined. Many times, when I invite individuals, I am unaware of time pressures or, indeed, personal difficulties that rule them out from commitment to the programme, at least on this occasion. However, they always seemed delighted to be invited and to have the opportunity for discussion.

In all this process, there is something very important at work. You are forming relationships. You are engaging with people at the level of their spirit and generosity, and encouraging them to discern their giftedness. In this way, and through the invitation, they receive a clear message from you of what you think they are capable of. This may challenge them, in that they may not previously have considered themselves in this way. The process provides a foundation for good and healthy relationships.

I have dealt with group hosts at some length because of their importance in encouraging open discussion, forming a sense of being pilgrims together and mirroring discipleship in today's world. Essentially, their focus is on facilitating for each person a new or deeper relationship with Christ and affirming indications when they see this happening for individuals. Reviews of the programme suggest that the small group is a key place where people obtain the greatest personal help and benefit.

Training Hosts

The following is a suggested outline in training hosts. The number of meetings required depends on the needs of hosts and the extent to which they are engaged in their individual faith journey, Church belonging, commitment to evangelisation, faith sharing and spontaneous prayer. At the same time, one meeting may be sufficient, setting aside an extended period of time during a Saturday afternoon or a weekday evening.

1: Spontaneous Sharing and Prayer
Luke 5:1–11 is an excellent reading for reflection during the time of spontaneous sharing and prayer. It helps hosts to reflect on the task, and on personal attitudes towards, for example launching into the deep, knowing who the principal partner is, working together, recognising their own unworthiness, mission.

2: Hopes
It is good to outline your hopes for the programme. This brings clarity and unity of purpose. It is also important to allow time for agreed hopes to emerge. The following were my hopes for a recent *Inspiring Faith Communities* programme:
- That people grow in their relationship with the Lord and in the spirit of evangelisation (discipleship), and
- That people who wish may have the option to explore the formation of small parish communities on completion of the programme.

You adapt your hopes for the programme to suit your local situation. For example, you may hope that people will commit to evangelisation or to a particular ministry within the parish.

3: Overview of Programme and Meeting
In communicating a general overview of the programme, you can draw upon the outline and content of the six meetings. Then you inform the hosts of the format for each meeting.
- Introduction, welcome and scripture
- Presentation
- Personal testimony
- Tea, which presents an opportunity to chat
- Time for discussion in small groups

4: Preparatory and Review Meetings

These are important meetings for hosts and all involved in the organisation of the programme. I recommend that these people come together forty-five minutes prior to the beginning of each meeting. This gives them time to reflect and pray together and draw attention to practicalities, and builds community as people prepare to welcome participants.

Taking time with hosts for up to fifteen minutes after each meeting ends has great value. Hosts hear what happened in each group, and the issues raised. This builds confidence and affirmation. It also offers you the opportunity to respond.

5: Controversial Issues
I offer three suggestions for hosts in dealing with issues that are controversial.
- Accept what is said as an interesting contribution.
- Distinguish between what is personal and what is opinion.
- Discern whether it may be beneficial to meet with an individual outside the meeting. It usually is.

6: Prayer during Small Group Time
Perhaps it is best not to have prayer as part of the first meeting, as a number of participants may be far from the Church and have a nebulous or distant view of God. Then, during the second meeting, it may be introduced very simply as a moment of silence, which ends with Glory be to the Father, and to the Son, and to the Holy Spirit. Amen. During subsequent meetings, gently encourage a spirit of spontaneous prayer.

Final Comments
Hosts are setting out on their own journeys of renewal and self-discovery. They are also embarking on being spiritual leaders and offering leadership as missionary disciples. A few brief comments

by the overall convenor about what this means and involves will greatly clarify their role. It is essentially service, and in the context of this programme, they encourage participants to talk and have good conversations. Hosts need to listen carefully, and not respond with answers to every issue raised. An emphasis on confidentiality is always relevant. This means that nothing is said that identifies a participant, not even during the review meetings, except when professional advice is necessary.

Launching into something new, which you suspect has immense possibilities, is exciting and also daunting. Each journey begins with a single step. The destination may appear to be far away, but we will certainly never arrive without setting out. We will make mistakes. What we do will be imperfect. As Karl Rahner said, 'In the torment of the insufficiency of everything attainable, we come to understand here in this life, all symphonies remain unfinished.' You are beginning an exciting journey with others. Your task and privilege is to point them towards the Lord so that they may know his love and the unique activity of his Holy Spirit. It deserves your best preparation.

The following sections carry the theme, format and resources of each presentation, as well as comments for best use during preparation and pafter meetings. It needs to be remembered that the resources serve as guidelines. The intention here is that each presenter will internalise the theme and content, and use the resources as a catalyst to access his or her own resources. I also suggest that you draw upon your own creativity, and/or that of others, in the provision of music, reflection and ritual at the beginning and end of each meeting.

First Meeting

God's Longing for Us

Preparatory Meeting

Hosts gather and sit in a circle. Very briefly, outline the format, content and theme of the meeting. Try to ensure that this meeting begins and ends on time. This highlights the importance of a timekeeper for both preparatory meetings and programme. The meeting has three sections.

1: Scripture/Prayer/Worship (10–15 minutes)
  a) A volunteer reads Matthew 6:25–34, which is the scripture for the meeting.
  b) Those present quietly reflect on, and are present to, God's word.
  c) After a few moments, give the hosts the option of reading a phrase or sentence that has meaning for them.
  d) Encourage those who wish to put into words a spontaneous prayer.
  e) A hymn and/or brief prayer may begin this section, while another hymn may be part of the time of spontaneous prayer and worship.

2: Information (10 minutes approximately)
Explain how groups will be organised, and where they will be located, and that hosts will be assigned during the coffee/tea break when the number attending is known.

When groups form, the host(s) will briefly and informally introduce themselves, using their Christian names, and saying what they look forward to during this programme and what their hopes are for each person present.

The hosts may find some or all of the following questions helpful during the time of group discussion:

- How did you hear about *Inspiring Faith Communities*? What prompted you to come?
- What did the presentation you just heard mean to you?
- Did it help you to think about yourself and your own journey? Can you explain?
- Did you find the scripture comforting, consoling, challenging? Would you like to say more (if answer is 'yes')?
- Do you wish to make any comment about all that has happened here?

These suggestions are offered simply to facilitate conversation and discussion that will be informal and build a spirit of community. They are also intended to evoke personal responses. Some people, at least during the initial few meetings, tend to avoid what is personal and speak about problems and solutions in the Church or in society, and even offer advice about or correct what another has said. The important thing here is that the host is aware of what is happening and gently seeks to evoke responses that are personal.

Alert hosts to be aware that some who attend may be very distant from God and his people; some may carry great burdens and difficulties and are urgently seeking meaning in life; a number may have found it hard to decide to come; and for many it may be the first time that they did anything like this to deepen their faith. For all of them, this is a providential moment when God wishes to surprise them and do a new work in their lives.

This perspective is intended to encourage in the hosts an understanding and sympathetic heart, respect and welcome for each person and each contribution, and a conviction that God is with them and among them. This is also a good time to remind them to find some helpful way of remembering the name of each person as she or he arrives for the next meeting; in this way, as hosts, they will communicate their interest in them.

Your final words to them might be; 'Enjoy the conversations. Be yourselves. You are with fellow pilgrims. God is among you.'

3: Arrival (20 minutes)

People may already be arriving. On arrival, name tags are given to each individual, and their names are taken. Those involved in hospitality are at their posts about twenty minutes prior to the official starting time, and will communicate a genuine welcome to participants. Hosts can mingle among them to greet them and chat with them as they see fit, without pretence or affectation.

Welcome

This is not a time for great explanations or overviews of what will happen during the next six weeks. People simply need the assurance that they have come to a friendly and safe place. It may take only two or three minutes, yet it sets a 'tone' for the rest of the night. A friendly, chatty and informal approach that conveys a genuine appreciation that people have come, is best.

It greatly helps those attending when the person who welcomes communicates some indication of the influence of God in his or her own life, perhaps with a reference to the purpose or meaning of *Inspiring Faith Communities*. Again, this can be presented in an informal and simple way. An example from life can be very striking. On one occasion, I heard the person who introduced the meeting speak briefly about being in a flower shop that day. She looked at a hyacinth flower in its early stages and began to reflect on how beautiful it will become as its petals open outwards. She connected this image with her hopes that during this programme God would help each person to flower and open out so that she or he would come to know his or her beauty and enjoy a new freedom. Alternatively, the introduction may be centred on a very simple ritual, which provokes a spirit of reflection and hope.

The person who will proclaim the scriptures is now introduced, as well as the one who will give the teaching. The scriptures are then proclaimed. Invite silence as a response. At this stage, people seem to welcome a time of silence. It gives them a moment to 'draw breath'. It need be no more than a minute or two. This 'breath' also creates a receptive space into which God's word is proclaimed and heard.

Resources for Presentation

The resources detailed below are intended to help you to prepare to make a presentation of not more than twenty minutes' duration. They are not intended as a presentation or talk to be closely followed but rather, as you make them your own, as an encouragement to recall and draw upon your own resources and stories.

Whenever I give this talk in the *Inspiring Faith Communities* series, I begin by communicating a sense that we (participants, hosts and organisers) are setting out on a journey together. We each carry our own stories. We have travelled our unique paths in life. Together we carry such a great variety and richness, and now we set out together.

Is it really about *our* journey? Is it solely our search, our longing for freedom, for God? If yes, then we remain largely in control. We think that as we find help, we can work things out for ourselves. In this way, we remain in the driving seat as we journey onwards.

Or is it God's longing for us that is at work here? If yes, then there will be moments when he surprises us, when we feel he finds us and draws us into his embrace, and when we know his personal love and providence.

Personal Story

I recommend that the person making the presentation speaks about an example(s) when God surprised him or her. This has the effect of 'incarnating' and 'grounding' the Christian story and making it concrete for listeners. It attunes them to recognise surprises of God in their experiences of life, which they may, or may not, have named in this way. It also draws attention to God's active involvement in their personal history and opens them to his influence. In the booklet *Living Word*, guidelines are given to help people write stories from their personal histories about where they have seen the imprint of God's goodness and wisdom. I now give a personal example, which I used a number of times when I was asked to make this first presentation on 'God's Longing for Us'.

My first appointment included teaching, being chaplain to religious sisters, and managing a youth club in Dublin's inner city. This last role led me to visit quite a few families. I came face to face with life in the tenements. The interiors of the homes I visited were warm and welcoming. People were warm-hearted, earthy and gracious, yet so much else spoke of poverty – especially the cold approaches of the flats and tenements. I remember one cold November evening as I visited I heard the wind howling through the tenement stairways. It stopped me in my tracks and I asked myself: Is there something more that I should be giving these people beyond what I am doing? What am I supposed to do? Would a social worker be more effective? Is this what my life as a priest is all about? Should I expect more from being a priest? Who, indeed, is God to me in this situation?

Little did I know that God was about to surprise me and begin a major change in my life. I was twenty-six years of age at that time. I happened to receive a copy of *Bury Me in My Boots* by Sally Trench, who had pioneered the Samaritans in London. In her book she speaks about suffering from burnout. She says that during her illness she realised she had been working *for* God; henceforth, she decided to work *with* him.

Her thought got me really thinking. Even though I did not fully understand it, I too knew I had been working for a distant God. I now wished I could work with God. I began to read widely in order to understand what this might mean. Mostly, I read books about prayer and about people whom God had surprised and transformed. I talked to people about what was happening to me.

I had a lot of questions. What would I be like if I followed this route? Would I become a religious fanatic or, perhaps worse, would I be seen as one? I could easily have said 'no'. I did not phrase it in that way. I kept wondering whether I was somewhat mad. For some reason, I went with what seemed to be drawing me onwards. Now I know it was God's way of speaking to me. He was surprising me.

During the following eighteen months, I gradually came to see God in a very different way. He was near. He was in me. He was inviting me to a deeper relationship with him. I could now take my questions and anxieties to him and expect his wisdom for my path in life.

I also realised that I needed people. I was attracted to places where I could hear their prayer and reflection. I needed to hear their prayer with and for me. All this was simply for my own support and encouragement. In time, I realised the importance of having a small faith group of people with whom I could share in this way. This led me in time to pioneer small evangelising communities (which we call parish cell communities) in Ireland. Little did I realise the surprises and challenges God had in mind for me when, many years previously, I struggled with fundamental questions of priesthood, ministry and God.

Francis Thompson (1859–1907)

The truth is that God pursues each of us and wishes to surprise us. Francis Thompson is a well-known English poet. He grew up in Preston, Lancashire. He was educated at Ushaw College and then studied medicine at Owens College, now the University of Manchester. He had no interest in his studies and never practised as a doctor. Instead he moved to London, with hopes of becoming a writer.

He soon became an opium addict and began living on the streets at Charing Cross and sleeping by the River Thames with the homeless and other addicts. It is known that he attempted suicide at least once. Then, in 1888, after one of his poems was discovered, he was helped to leave penury and self-destruction behind.

'The Hound of Heaven', his best-known poem, may be described as his journey from desperation to freedom. In its opening verses, he tells of his flight from God. He sought to silence God in the varied activities of life, he says. For many years, by day and night, he simply kept going to escape from God. He was caught up in his own rationalisations and excuses. Even in the midst of complexities, he continued to run and 'hide' from God.

> I fled Him, down the nights and down the days;
> I fled Him, down the arches of the years;
> I fled Him, down the labyrinthine ways
> Of my own mind; and in the midst of tears
> I hid from Him, and under running laughter.

Yet, all the time, Thompson was being pursued. He describes his pursuer as a hound, confident in power, graceful in movement, unhurried in progress and deliberate in majesty.

> From those strong Feet that followed, followed after
> But with unhurrying chase,
> And unperturbed pace,
> Deliberate speed, majestic instancy

Thompson was caught in a dilemma. He knew he was not alone and that a divine Love pursued him. However, he feared to accept it.

> (For, though I knew His love Who followed,
> Yet was I sore adread
> Lest, having Him, I must have naught beside).

Eventually, his pursuer, 'this tremendous Lover', speaks to him. He tells Thompson that his unworthiness (and his life) does not keep such great love at a distance. He comes with a perfect love to find and rescue him, and to invite him to arise to new beginnings.

> How little worthy of any love thou art!
> Whom wilt thou find to love ignoble thee,
>   Save Me, save only Me? …
> Rise, clasp My hand, and come!

Dorothy Day (1987–1980)

Dorothy Day was an American journalist and social activist. 'The Hound of Heaven' equally tells her story. 'This tremendous Lover' also surprised her. Day got caught up in the Jazz Age's sexual revolution. She had a love affair with a hard-drinking writer during her early twenties. She had an abortion, married a man while on the rebound, and decided to live for a year in Europe. Her marriage broke up, and she later bore a daughter out of wedlock with another man. She says that holding her baby and looking into her face had a profound effect on her. She said she simply felt the 'longing to thank someone' for her experience and for her child. Then, in December 1927, she surrendered to the incessant 'Hound of Heaven'. She tells us how and when this happened.

> I was traveling and far from home and lonely, and I awoke in the night almost on the verge of weeping with a sense of futility, of being unloved and unwanted. And suddenly the thought came to me of my importance as a daughter of God, daughter of a King, and I felt a sureness of God's love. And I felt a sureness of God's love and at the same time a conviction that one of the greatest injustices, if one can put it that way, which one can do to God is to distrust his love, not realise his love. God so loved me that he gave his only begotten son. 'If a mother shall forget her children,

never will I forget thee.' Such tenderness, and with such complete ingratitude we forget the Father and his love![75] This surprising intervention led her to enter the Catholic Church. She went on to establish the Catholic Worker Movement. She lived the rest of her live without income or security. She spent every effort to shelter the homeless, speak out against injustice, violence and war and spread a radical understanding of God's merciful love, especially through her writings and her life's witness. Many believe she will one day be declared a saint. An unlikely saint, we can add, when we consider her earlier years! It points to the grace and surprises of God.

C. S. Lewis (1898–1963)

Clive Staples Lewis was a novelist, academic, literary critic, lay theologian and Christian apologist. In *Surprised by Joy: The Shape of My Early Life* (1955), Lewis tells about growing up in Belfast and about how faith was passed on to him. He was taught prayers, he says, but there was little emphasis on religion. When he went to college, he completely left religions behind and became a 'convinced atheist'. He claims, however, that all the time something kept pulling at him. It felt like the presence of God. He tried to ignore it as it came and went. He did not pay it much attention.

Then one day something happened. This is how he describes it: 'You must picture me alone in that room in Oxford College, feeling the steady, unrelenting approach of Him whom I earnestly desired not to meet. It was in 1929 that I gave in, and admitted that God was God and I knelt and I prayed, perhaps that night, the most dejected and reluctant convert in all of England.'[76]

This event was to change his life. While Lewis described himself as a 'reluctant convert', what happened challenged him, his thinking, his standards, his life. Many years of deep and intense questioning followed. Finally, after much discussion, searching and prayer, he

75 David Scott, *The Catholic Passion – Rediscovering the Power and Beauty of the Faith*, Chicago, IL: Loyola Press, 2005, 32. Scott writes of Day in the chapter entitled 'God, the Hound of Heaven'.
76 Roger White, Judith Wolfe and Brendan N. Wolfe, *C. S. Lewis – His Circle Essays and Memoirs of the C S Lewis Society*, Oxford: Oxford University Press: 2015, 6, 199.

came to a friendship with God that was personal and real, and which engaged him. He came to see God in all things and in the wonder of each moment. He was indeed surprised by God, and by his epic pursuit.

St Augustine (354–430)

The life of St Augustine gives us another great example of God's pursuing love, which surprises. It is a story that in part is about resisting conversion. The attraction of the world was too strong for Augustine, even though he had gradually become convinced of the truth of Christianity through the prayers of his mother Monica, hearing the story of St Anthony of the Desert, reading St Paul's letter to the Romans (chapters 12–15) and the influence of St Ambrose. He continued to say, 'Soon, in a little while, I shall make up my mind, but not right now.' He also reproached himself, 'And Thou, O Lord, how long? How long? Is it to be tomorrow and tomorrow? Why not now? Why not this very hour put an end to shame?'

Finally, Augustine yielded to God's great love. Months later, during Easter 387, and after preparation, he was baptised by St Ambrose in the presence of St Monica, together with Adeodatus, his son, and Alipius, a friend. We know St Augustine's prayer of conversion:

> Too late, have I loved Thee, O Beauty so ancient and so new, too late have I loved Thee! Thou wast with me, and I was not with Thee; I was abroad, running after those beauties which Thou hast made; those things, which could have no being but in Thee, kept me away from Thee. Thou hast called, Thou hast cried out, and hast pierced my deafness. Thou hast enlightened, Thou hast shone forth, and my blindness is dispelled. I have tasted Thee, and am hungry for Thee. Thou hast touched me, and I am afire with the desire of thy embraces.[77]

77 St Augustine, *Confessions* (Book 7,10, 18; 10, 27).

Matthew 6:25–34

This is the scripture reading that was read towards the beginning of the meeting. During this presentation, it is highly recommended to make connections with it, however brief.

This is, for some people, their favourite scripture passage. It speaks to the restless spirit and the anxious heart. It tells us about divine providence. It describes God who is eager to provide for us. It brings us face to face with personal worry and how we can best deal with it. It invites us to look at nature and to see its patterns. The birds of the air possess a beauty much greater than the splendour of Solomon. I recently heard a story of a father who, as he worked in his garden, explained to his young daughter, 'I plant the seed. I water it. But then I wait for God to give the growth.' She declared that his words left such an impression on her that, whenever she remembers them, they deepen her trusting faith in God.

This scripture reveals God's commitment to our well-being and his concern for the details of life. He knows when a sparrow falls from a rooftop. He feeds the birds and grows the flowers. There is nothing too small that he does not notice and continues to create. The Father has numbered every hair on our heads, or, for some of us, he sees how many have already fallen away. He knows when we are hungry and naked. He is concerned about how we are to be nourished and clothed. We can indeed trust that he will provide us with all we need.

Scripture is rich in examples of God's love and his interventions, which surprise. We see his love when he calls people to follow him, and when he speaks to them, feeds them and heals them. An outstanding example of a love and an intervention that surprises is the story of the conversion of St Paul, as described in Acts 9:3–19; 22:6–21; 26:12–18. These extracts can be very beneficial resources for the person presenting this talk.

Everything comes from love. (St Catherine of Siena)

You cannot imagine at all how much you interest God; he is interested in you as if there were no one else on earth. (French writer Julien Green)

Finding the lost sheep is a joy to God, because he has a 'loving weakness' for those who are lost. ... The work of God is to 'go and search', in order to 'invite everyone to the celebrations. He can't stand losing one of his own. He is a God who walks around searching for us, and has a certain loving weakness for those who are furthest away, who are lost. He goes and searches for them. And how does he search? He searches until the end, like the shepherd who goes out into the darkness, searching, until he finds the sheep. Or like the woman, when she loses a coin, who lights a lamp and sweeps the house, and searches carefully. This is our Father: he always comes searching for us. (Pope Francis, Rome, 7 November 2013)

The drama of God's pursuit of us is also the story of our hiding from him, our failure to know his love. Try as we might, however, we can never elude him. The best we can do is delude ourselves that we have given him the slip. Like it or not, we are made for God.

If we too stop and pause amid the frenetic rush of today's living, as Dorothy Day did, we will also hear the voice of God, promising to fill us with the love we long for. We will hear him pleading with us in the words of Thompson's poem:

Whom wilt thou find to love ignoble thee,
Save Me, save only Me

Alternatively, this presentation can be made in two parts. The first part (10–12 minutes) comprises a teaching of God's longing for us and draws upon some of the resources detailed above. Another person presents the second part (10 minutes) in the form of a personal story of witness where she or he gives example(s) of the theme – of the longing of God who intervenes and surprises us – from the concrete situations of his or her life.

Tea or coffee follows the presentation. In the meantime, a number has been assigned to each circle. At the end of the tea break an announcement is made about the formation of small groups and that those with numbers assigned to them as they arrived will now go to their numbered group. Circles are formed for discussion. The time of discussion ends with an announcement about how to use the booklet (*Living Word*) as a basis for daily prayer and reflection. There follows a reference to next week, its theme and who the speaker(s) is. Participants then depart.

Review Meeting
The hosts gather and sit in a circle. Each has the option of making a brief review of their discussion time; of why people came; the spirit of participation; particular hopes and fears; and any outstanding feature. This is often a rather difficult night for participants and hosts, with each having a sense of going into the unknown. Usually there is a great sense of joy (and relief) at what has happened. Hosts will usually feel surprised by an awareness of God's help.

Thoughts then turn to the second meeting and to practical issues that need to be addressed. In summing up, and in looking ahead, thank the hosts for their work and openness; encourage them to place their trust in God's Spirit and to pray for the participants in their group; and lead them to expect Christ to do a great work in each person. The meeting ends with a prayer and/or hymn. This review meeting lasts fifteen minutes at most.

Second Meeting

Why Did Jesus Come?

Preparatory Meeting
This follows the same format, with similar elements and time allotment as during the previous meeting.

1: Scripture/prayer/worship
Luke 4:16–22 is the scripture reading for this meeting. Invite a volunteer to read it as a basis for reflection, prayer and worship. Create an atmosphere where people may respond or pray spontaneously as they wish. Remember that it takes time for such a response to develop.

2: Information
What is communicated will reflect feedback from the previous meeting. It is good to remind hosts of a number of things:
- that the Spirit of God is with them and that he is at work in each participant;
- to be alert to silent and quiet people; this is the individual's choice. A role of the host is to create a welcoming and encouraging spirit among all within the group;
- to be alert to people who may dominate within the group; depending on feedback already received, it may be good, even necessary, to discuss what may help where there is a dominant person;
- to model responses for others in the group – in other words, to share briefly and in a personal way, and be

genuinely eager to hear what others wish to say;

- to be aware of tangents that go nowhere. This can be important, as they justdetract from communicating in a personal way and may even be a way of avoiding doing so;
- to encourage listening to one another, as a way of showing respect to fellow participants;
- to speak about the value of confidentiality within their small group;
- to introduce prayer as a feature of the group. It may be no more than inviting a brief time of silence and ending with a very brief prayer, which may be traditional or spontaneous;
- to pray for the participants in their group;
- to agree who will play the more prominent leading role during this meeting. This applies when there are two hosts assigned to the same discussion group.

Some of the following questions may be helpful to prompt discussion. However, it is worth remembering that as people sit down they may wish to engage immediately in a personal way with the presentations. This is to be encouraged.

- How are you since last week?
- Tell us what you heard in the presentation/story. What did you find interesting?
- Share an image, or images, you may have of the Lord Jesus.
- Tell us who Jesus is to you now.
- Talk about how and when you came to see him and relate to him in this way.
- Did anyone use the little booklet during the week? How did you find it? Has anyone a question to ask?

3: *Arrival*

Each host now goes towards the location where they will meet with the small group assigned to them during the previous meeting. Each waits to greet and welcome the group participants as they arrive.

Welcome

The welcome communicates a genuine joy at being together again. An informal attitude and words express a joyful welcome. Newcomers are, in a general way, specifically welcomed. It can be very salient to share a personal reflection or story that emerged during the past week, for example an instance when the speaker became aware of God's love and concern, or one that briefly tells who Jesus has become for him or her. This also has the effect of creating a link with the previous meeting, or with the forthcoming presentation.

Then the scripture, Luke 4:16–22, is proclaimed (perhaps by the host who has already read it during the preparatory meeting). There follows a reflective space.

Resources for Presentation

Last week, we looked at the love God has for us and for all people, as he provides for, pursues and surprises us. This week we take a look at the lengths God went to as he revealed his love for us in Jesus. This is a crucially important presentation during the programme.

This presentation can be undertaken in one of two ways, and is best when it lasts less than 25 minutes. The first option addresses the theological understanding of why Jesus came, and of what redemption means. This needs to be achieved in a rather simplified way because thinking in this way may be new for many participants. Then a second person responds to the content of what has been said by speaking briefly about some of the ways people see Jesus and then telling the story of who he has come to mean in their own experience. This includes speaking about the circumstances that led to this new understanding and giving examples of Jesus' current personal impact upon the speaker.

The second option is that the same speaker addresses the two aspects of this presentation. She or he presents some theological insights and then proceeds to tell the story of how Jesus has revealed his personal presence and love, and the impact of this revelation for the individual.

The first option has advantages in that different voices and experiences are heard. I have seen it being most effective when a young person speaks about Jesus becoming a real friend. This option demands a good discipline in terms of time. The second option has an advantage in that it reveals how both theological and personal strands run together in one person's experience. It is important that the total speaking time is less than twenty-five minutes, irrespective of which option is taken.

A good place to begin is to highlight some incorrect images of Jesus, salvation and redemption. The presenter may give first-hand, even personal examples. An image, encouraged by some devotional practices, is that Jesus was nailed to the cross by our sins, and that every personal sin continues to contribute to his pain. This has the effect of inducing guilt. Another incorrect image is that of an angry father who demanded the death of his son. I remember this image being explained to me as a child to help me understand why Jesus died. It made me somewhat suspicious of God.

Scripture gives us some very different images. Our reading at the beginning of this presentation, for example, introduces us to what we can name as the mission statement of Jesus. Here he announces that he is chosen for the specific purpose of bringing good news to the poor, liberty to captives, recovery of sight to the blind and freedom for the oppressed. He is God actively present for the good of people and the world. He announces a vision of a new world, inspires hope for all who are poor, captive, blind and oppressed, and dispels our fear and despair.

As Jesus announces his mission, he seeks our engagement at a personal level. He invites us to travel with him the path of announcing good news to the poor. He does not look to us to be bystanders and observers of life, but to commit to alleviating poverty and oppression. At the same time, he invites us to a still more personal engagement. He desires to be for us good news proclaimed within the crevices of our darkness and loneliness; release from our patterns of acting and from substances that hold us addicted; vision beyond our pettiness and self-centredness; and our freedom beyond what oppresses and depresses us. We are to know and welcome him as God's saving love at work in us and then through us among his people.

Scripture tells us that love inspired the coming and death of Jesus: 'Yes, God loved the world so much that he gave his only Son, so that everyone who believes in him may not be lost but may have eternal life. For God sent his Son into the world not to condemn the world, but so that through him the world might be saved' (Jn 3:16–17). We find many other references throughout scripture, which state that love is the purpose of the coming of Jesus, for example Mt 9:12–13; Mt 18:11–14; Mk 2:17; Lk 5:30–32: Lk 19:10; Gal 4:4–7; 1 Jn 4:10.

The Garden of Eden and Life Beyond
A chatty, graphic and imaginative way of presenting the story of the Garden of Eden, the Fall and Redemption leaves a great impact upon participants. It could begin with a description of an idyllic life in the best of gardens. Indeed, this single theme could be developed with great creative imagination to revolve around a number of gardens and open spaces.

Genesis chapter one presents in metaphorical imagery and language God's gradual creating of the world. It includes the creation of day and night; seas and dry land; vegetation – plants and trees; sun and moon; birds and sea creatures; finally, cattle, reptiles and every kind of wild beast. God saw them and declared it good.

In Genesis chapter two, we read that Yahweh fashioned man out of dust from the soil. Then he breathed into his nostrils a breath of life, and thus man became a living being. Then Yahweh God made man fall into a deep sleep, and while man slept, the story tells us, Yahweh God took one of his ribs and enclosed it in flesh. He built the rib he had taken from the man into a woman.

Genesis is not intended as a description of how creation actually came to be, but rather to draw attention to our humble origins and the beauty of God's creating and call. It presents us with the real plan of God for us. Having all. All is given. All is received. God's intention was that we would have the best of fruit, the best of water and a place of pure gold, and so we are given a scenario in which our original parents danced together. Now both of them were naked, but they felt no shame in front of each other. God did not say they were good after he had created them. Could it be that he already foresaw that they would cause him much trouble? Their suspicion and disobedience led to their expulsion.

First was their suspicion. Perhaps this is not true. Perhaps we should test it for ourselves. Perhaps we will truly live when we taste it. We will no longer be subservient. Perhaps … we gain our freedom. No one tells us what we should or should not do, they argued.

Then shame entered. They realised they were naked so they hid from God, from each another. They could no longer look at each other with trust. They hid from God and wanted to keep him at a distance. Something major had been damaged in their circumstances and in the way they related to one another and to God.

They were expelled from the garden, with pain in childbearing, thistles and brambles; with sweat on their brow they will toil for a living and return to dust through death.

And then it became worse: Cain killed Abel. The Garden of Harmony and Fruitfulness became a place of suspicion, shame, disobedience, toil and death. That was now going to be the lot of all people.

But God, we read, said it can't end like this. After a meeting in heaven, he went on a long journey in search of a fallen humanity. He had a rescue package in mind. Scripture tells us, 'God loved the world so much that he gave his only Son ... that the world might be saved through him' (Jn 3:16–17). Sending Jesus was the revealing of love. Love motivated his coming. Jesus revealed his love by the way he related to people, and in giving his life for all.

Jesus entered many a garden. He was let by the spirit into the wilderness above Jericho for forty days (Lk 4:1–13). He was tempted. He was challenged to follow the way of

- popularity – turn these stones into bread and you will win many friends.
- power – use your miraculous power and throw yourself down from the parapet of the temple.
- possessions – I will give you all this land with its riches if, falling down, you will honour me.

Jesus turned his back on popularity, power and possessions. In this way it became clearer than ever to him that he was called to worship the Lord his God and serve him alone. He learned that a person is not to live on bread alone but on every word that comes from the mouth of God. He identified, in this way, with all who are tempted and succumb to these three attractions. He also offered a way out.

He entered the Garden of Gethsemane. He rested on a rock. His anguish was so intense that he sweated pools of blood. It was the anguish of seeing and carrying all the sin of the world.

He was led to Golgotha. He no longer had his freedom. All choice had been taken away. For him, 'my meat is to do the will of him who sent me'. Love was his way. He revealed a love that was divine and gave until he had nothing more to give. In him we see the nothingness of love – a love that gave to the end.

"It is finished." Then he bowed his head he gave up his spirit' (Jn 19:30). He bowed his head and died. A disgrace, the ultimate sign of failure, not popular, without power, without possessions. Here is a God who fails. A God who falls. We would have looked for a strong leader who wins and calls us all to be winners.

At this point my imagination fails. I can't imagine the dynamics of that moment. All I know is that scripture tells us that he was raised up at the right hand of the Father. 'He was humbler yet, even to accepting death, death on a cross. But God raised him high and gave him a name that is above all other names ... so that every tongue should acclaim Jesus Christ as lord to the glory of God the Father (Phil 2:8–9, 11). From the intimacy of the Father's love he continues to intercede for us now.

Through the resurrection of Jesus a new feature has been introduced into the world. It is as if a new energy has been released. Now at its core is the triumph of love. Jesus took on suspicion and mistrust and lived the opposite lifestyle, that of trusting and loving. In this way he turned back the clock. He triumphed over suffering, sin and death. In him, the boundaries that separated us from intimacy with God were shattered. In him, the boundaries that separated people from one another were destroyed.

The resurrection of Jesus is not simply an individual event in the life of Jesus. It is a corporate event. The world is changed for ever. It has, to put it graphically, been given a new DNA. The resurrection of Jesus, as a communal event, was, and remains, a strong theme in Orthodox Church theology. It points to a realignment of the principle of justice, namely, that at the end of time, there will be a balancing of justice and fairness for all. Thus injustice does not have the final word. Already we share in the triumph of justice in Jesus.

You can also draw upon other headings, categories of thinking and scriptural references. I suggest a few upon which you may find it helpful to reflect.

- Lamb of God – the Paschal Lamb. The blood of the lamb sprinkled on the doorposts led to freedom for the people of Israel. It meant that Moses was free to lead them out of slavery in Egypt towards freedom and the Holy Land (Ex 12:7).
- Scapegoat – animal sacrifices, 'the Lord has laid on him the iniquity of all' (Isa 53:6).

- Saved, Salvation – 'By his wounds you have been healed' (1 Pet 2:24).
- Forgiveness – God 'has rescued us from the power of darkness and transferred us into the kingdom of his beloved Son, in whom we have redemption, the forgiveness of sins' (Col 1:13–14).
- New Life – 'I have been crucified with Christ, and it is no longer I who live, but it is Christ who lives in me' (Gal 2:19–20).
- Good News – 'He has sent me to bring the good news to the poor, to proclaim liberty to captives, and to the blind new sight, to set the downtrodden free' (Lk 4:18).

Jesus came to bring life. 'I have come that they may have life, and have it abundantly' (Jn 10:10) sums up his plan, and the desire of his heart. His resurrected and victorious love is now fixed for all time towards us and in us. His rescue package is complete. At the same time, he invites our cooperation and participation in living the life that he offers us, he invites us all to come, follow him, and embrace the example he sets before us. 'Love one another as I have loved you' (Jn 15:12). He invites us to love in the same manner as he has loved. He is not inviting us to come and have nice feelings and beautiful prayer. He does not even invite us to worship him. Rather, the core of his invitation can be interpreted as a question. 'Can you walk with me the journey of loving?' This is the journey to true freedom where only love matters.

The *Catechism of the Catholic Church* expresses the saving mission of Jesus in the following way. The Word became flesh for us in order to save us by reconciling us with God, who 'loved us and sent his Son to be the expiation for our sins'; 'the Father has sent his Son as the Saviour of the world', and 'he was revealed to take away sins'.[78]

78   *CCC*, 457.

In the Words of Pope Francis

I include a number of quotes from Pope Francis, which are relevant to understanding the saving work of Jesus.

> On the lips of the catechist the first proclamation must ring out over and over: Jesus Christ loves you; he gave his life to save you, and now he is living at your side every day to enlighten, strengthen and free you. (*JG*, 164)

> A man has made sin; a man comes to heal it. God does not save us only through a decree, a law; he saves us with tenderness, he saves with caresses, he saves us with His life, for us. (Casa Sancta Marta, 22 October 2013)

> It is important that we let ourselves encounter the Lord: He always seeks us. He is always near us. Many times, though, we look the other way because we do not want to talk with the Lord or allow ourselves to encounter the Lord. Meeting the Lord [is important], but more importantly, let us be met by the Lord: this is a grace. (Casa Sancta Marta, 16 December 2013)

> God did not wait for everyone to go to Him, but it was he who moved towards us, without calculating, without measure. God is like this: He always takes the first step, He moves towards us. (General Audience, St Peter's, 27 March 2013).

I have on occasion employed one or more of the following three stories to bring into focus the mission of Jesus and the significance of his life of loving for us today. You may also find them helpful.

Under God's Wings

After a forest fire in Yellowstone National Park, largely in Wyoming, forest rangers went up a mountain to assess the damage caused by the raging inferno. One ranger found a bird with its flesh totally burned, while its bones were upright with ashes around it on the ground at the base of a tree. To see the bird so charred he became somewhat sick while he gently knocked over the bird with his stick. As he did so, three tiny chicks scurried out from under their dead mother's wings. The loving mother, keenly aware of impending disaster, had carried her offspring to the base of the tree and had gathered them under her wings, instinctively knowing that the toxic smoke would rise. She could have flown to safety but had refused to abandon her babies. Then the blaze had arrived and the heat had scorched her small body. The mother remained steadfast ... because she was willing to die, so that those under the cover of her wings would live.

For all its poignancy, this image is still incomplete. Jesus did not remain dead. He is risen beyond death. His love and healing are not then simply limited to the people he met. Rather, they are fixed for all time. Raised up he is Lord of all life. He is present everywhere. He is released from the confines of being present in only one place at any given moment. He is our ultimate security. The Lord is our light and our help. Then with him whom shall we fear? We can echo the psalmist and say, 'He will cover you with His feathers, And under His wings you will find refuge' (Ps 91:4). Indeed, we find our life in him, in God's saving grace and mercy.

Maximilian Kolbe

In 1941 a prisoner escaped from Auschwitz. The sub-commander (Karl Fritzsch) ordered that ten other prisoners die by starvation in reprisal. Franciszek Gajowniczek (15 November 1901–13 March 1995), a Polish army sergeant, was one of those selected. When prisoner number 16670 heard Gajowniczek cry, 'My poor wife! My poor children! What will they do? I will never see them again', he offered himself instead. Maximilian Kolbe's exact words have been forgotten, but one version records them as, 'I am a Catholic priest from Poland; I would like to take his place, because he has a wife and children.' The switch was permitted, and after all his cellmates had died, Kolbe was put to death with an injection of carbolic acid. Maximilian Kolbe – a forty-seven-year-old Franciscan priest – died on 14 August 1941.

Gajowniczek lived until 1995. In 1972 he said, 'I want to express my thanks, for the gift of life.' In 1994 he said that so long as he has breath in his lungs, he would consider it his duty to tell people about the heroic act of love by Maximilian Kolbe. He spent the rest of his life telling his story. He was present in 1971 when Kolbe was beatified and in 1982 when he was canonised, when Pope John Paul II declared him 'The Patron Saint of Our Difficult Century'.

Les Misérables
The opening scenes of *Les Misérables* are epic. We meet Chaverre, an inspector driven by his commitment to the law, and Jean Valjean, the hero, who has been so long enslaved and mistreated that he thinks and behaves like a starving animal.

Valjean, released from captivity after twenty years' penal servitude, is homeless and penniless. He is given a place to stay, a fire to warm himself, hot food and a bed, by the local bishop. But Valjean still has the reflexes of a prison survivor. He steals silver from the house and makes off in the middle of the night. Arrested next day and dragged back to his benefactor by the uncompromising Chaverre, Valjean is looking at a harsh life sentence.

However, in an act of amazing benevolence, the bishop plays along with Valjean's story. He agrees that he gave the silver to the former inmate. He playfully grabs a couple of silver candlesticks and says he intended Valjean to have them as well. He then quietly tells Valjean that he now has a responsibility to make something of his life. The rest of the story is about how this act of trusting and selfless generosity slowly transforms and gives the ex-convict a new life and sense of purpose.

Testimony of Faith

Personal stories about how the speaker understands redemption and the Paschal Mystery are rich resources, and can help communicate insights. Alternatively, they can reveal our own simplistic, even fundamentalist thinking. When I was sixteen years of age, I read Frank Sheed's *Theology for Beginners*,[79] and considered that I knew exactly the nature and dynamics of the Trinity and the Paschal Mystery. What naivety! This contributed greatly to my decision to study for the priesthood. God calls us in strange ways! At the same time, speaking about times of development and growth when one's current understanding of the saving event of Jesus was formed, can greatly benefit *Inspiring Faith Communities* participants.

The maximum time for sharing a story or testimony of faith is ten to twelve minutes. It is generally most effective when the presentation has three sections. The first comprises brief references to images of Jesus that people have today. The second tells briefly of images that the speaker may have had. The third is the central part of the presentation. It tells of the relationship, with image(s), that the speaker now has with, and of, Jesus; when it began; the circumstances of its beginning; and its influence upon the speaker's current attitudes and lifestyle.[80] A tea break follows the presentation.

The meeting ends in the way that you consider best, with all departing directly from the small group, or with a formal ending, which may include something sung together.

---

79   Third edition, Michigan, OH: Servant Books, 1958.
80   Further information on writing one's personal story of faith is included as part of the fourth meeting.

Third Meeting

Friendship (*Oikos*) Evangelisation

Preparatory Meeting

This follows the same format as previous meetings. John 1:35–46 is read as a basis for reflection, spontaneous prayer and worship.

Some of the following questions may help prompt discussion. They are used only as the host deems them helpful. As people are seated, they may, for example, wish to speak in a personal way about the presentation, and how it applies to them. This is to be encouraged.

- How are you since we last met?
- Does anyone wish to respond to what you have heard? What did you find interesting?
- Do you find the booklet helpful? Does it help you to pray? Explain in what way it has helped.
- Do you find it easy to set aside time for prayer and reflection each day? Explain.
- Does anyone wish to say what this evening has meant for you?

It may be beneficial to draw attention to issues raised during the previous meeting, and also to encourage prayer within the small groups. The meeting disperses and hosts go to their assigned area to greet and welcome the people in their group.

Welcome

Taking a welcoming and conversational approach, the person who introduces the meeting may wish to speak about a scriptural passage by which he or she was greatly influenced, or a personal event that revealed the presence of Jesus and deepened trust in his promises and providence. The scripture is proclaimed, as in previous meetings, and is followed by a time of silence.

Resources for Presentation

This presentation has two sections. The first is a theological reflection on the theme of evangelisation as related to relationships, friendships and extended family. I recommend that it shouldn't last more than ten to twelve minutes. The resources below are intended to help in preparing to present this section. The second section presents the same theme in the form of telling a story that is personal and related to concrete and personal attitudes and events. It seems best when it doesn't last more than fifteen minutes. The two sections overlap somewhat. Two people may be involved during this presentation.

I Have No Other Plans

S. D. Gordon has a beautiful story about the ascension of Jesus into heaven. When the grand welcome ceremony was over, the angel Gabriel approached Jesus to address his doubts. He said, 'I know that only very few in Palestine are aware of the great work of human salvation you have accomplished through your suffering, death and resurrection. But the whole world should know and appreciate it and become your disciples, acknowledging you as their Lord and Saviour. What is your plan of action?' Jesus answered, 'I have told all my apostles to tell other people about me and preach my message through their lives. That's all.' 'Suppose they don't do that?' Gabriel asked. 'What's your Plan B?' Jesus replied, 'I have no other plan; I am counting on them.' A central conclusion from this story is that Jesus is counting on each participant and Christian believer to make him known, loved and accepted by others around them.

I wonder to what extent we are convinced of this. I am not sure I am convinced of it. In many respects we have the best secret society in the world and keep our good news to ourselves. I read one survey that claims that only about 2 per cent of Catholics have a genuine desire to share faith with other people. Yes, faith is generally important to those who believe. They are anxious to 'keep' it. However, they are hesitant about 'giving' it away, and hence it tends to remain a private comfort, especially during times of struggle. In the meantime, they leave it to specialists and others to witness to it before other people. An example for me is that parents recently invited me to approach teachers so that they would teach their children their basic prayers.

The question now becomes how we might most effectively evangelise in our context. The scripture reading for this meeting (Jn 1:35–46) highlights the relational nature of evangelisation as brother invited brother, and friend and neighbour invited friend and neighbour to 'come and see' Jesus. It is, no doubt, included in John's Gospel because the early followers of Jesus saw that they had come to see and know him principally through the invitation of a family member, neighbour or friend. It is also included because the early followers of Jesus recognised that this also corresponded to the method of Jesus. While he often spoke to the crowds, he spent most of his time in a more personal setting with a few friends or with an individual. Moreover, scripture gives us many examples when he called people as individuals to follow him. Therefore, this passage from John indicates that, while evangelisation is a multi-faceted reality, and often complex, a preeminent opportunity for evangelisation exists when familial and one-to-one relationships and friendships are emphasised as channels of God's word. Is this to be a template for evangelisation for all time?

Evangelisation then happened naturally within the structures of life. In other words, it happened as an inevitable process of belonging to *oikos*, or extended family. *Oikos* is the Greek word for members of a household or the house where the household meets. It is used many times in the New Testament. Its first meaning is of greatest interest to us here. In Acts 10:24, Cornelius 'called together his relatives and close friends' (*oikos*) when Peter came to him. *Oikos* identifies the network of people with whom an individual relates on a regular basis – family, friends, neighbours, those at work and at school. *Oikos* evangelisation refers to the quality of those relationships. It sees that where there is genuine concern and love for another, and where trust exists, these daily networks are the most effective places of ministry. They become the natural means of witness and evangelisation, expressed through personal example, conversation, listening and faith sharing. This background also explains why *oikos* evangelisation is often referred to as friendship or relational evangelisation.

We may be tempted to think that parish evangelisation is achieved when we celebrate good liturgies, get the right priest, organise a mission, run a programme or take on a particular initiative. Each of these contributes greatly in its own way. However, as I recently read a number of studies based in the USA, I came to see a largely untapped potential on the part of the Church in leading others to Christ, namely, the individual Christian. The surveys, I read, estimate that, on average, about 85 per cent of those who return to the Church, and to a deeper faith, do so at the invitation of a friend, neighbour or family member. These findings indicate the evangelical influence of a personal invitation issued by one person to another when trust exists between them. For me, they point to the necessity for providing training and formation to every believer so that they can invite, share faith and evangelise within the relational and informal settings in which they live. Incidentally, these surveys estimate that the priest tends to influence about 6 per cent, or less, of those who return to the Church or to a deeper faith.

Oikos evangelisation is based on the reality that we tend to meet the same people each day. They are most notably from within our family, neighbourhood and arenas of work and leisure. In these relational and friendship settings there exist daily opportunities to love, serve, listen to and pray for others and to share our values and faith. We thus don't have to go anywhere to evangelise, we evangelise as we go. These settings provide opportunities for interacting at the levels of meaning and faith, and for prayer, debate and aftercare. They are natural settings for storytelling where participants naturally talk about what enriches them. They can also be very challenging settings because we tend to withhold from others what is personal about our values and faith. We may suspect that sharing at this level involves too great a risk. However, this amounts to a failure in loving in that we withhold what can greatly enrich another.

Alcoholics Anonymous estimates that each alcoholic affects at least eight people for the worst in a significant way. Is it not equally true then that each person may affect a similar number in relation to what brings goodness, and towards living a deeper faith, trust in God and a life of witness and worship? During this presentation, it may be helpful to reflect with participants on the extent to which one person may influence another, and to give personal examples of the influence of one or more people, through their lifestyle and words.

> All authority in heaven and on earth has been given to me. Go, therefore, make disciples of all nations, baptising them in the name of the Father and of the Son and of the Holy Spirit, and teaching them to obey everything I have commanded you. And remember, I am with you always, to the end of the age. (Mt 28:18–20)

> We wish to affirm once more that the essential mission of the Church is to evangelise all people. Evangelisation is the special grace and vocation of the church. It is her essential function. The Church exists to preach the Gospel. [81]

> The evangelising activity of the Christian community is the clearest sign of a mature faith. The effectiveness of the Church's organisations, movements, parishes and apostolic

---

81   *EN*, 14.

works must be measured in the light of this missionary imperative. Only by becoming missionary will the Christian community be able to overcome its internal divisions and tensions, and rediscover its unity and its strength of faith.[82]

A few years ago, Archbishop Diarmuid Martin emphasised that the Church simply cannot survive if Catholics do not tell their stories of what is important to them.

Evangelisation takes place as 'one beggar tells another beggar where good news is to be found'. (Mother Teresa)

There is nothing more beautiful than to be surprised
    by the Gospel,
by the encounter with Christ.
There is nothing more beautiful than to know him
And to speak to others of our friendship with Him.
(Pope Benedict XVI)[83]

Faith Story

The maximum time allotted here is usually fifteen minutes. The presenter tells in story form the meaning and experience of *oikos*, and how she or he has learned faith within its friendship, relational and familiar settings, and in turn has shared, and shares, faith within his or her primary relationships.

The presenter may equally speak about a time when she or he finds it difficult to share faith within the household, while at the same time continuing to pray that she or he may one day have such an opportunity to do so as an exchange of love.

A tea break follows the presentation before the small group conversations. The ending is as in previous meetings.

---

82 *RM*, 48.
83 From Pope Benedict XVI's homily at his Mass of Inauguration, April 2005.

Fourth Meeting

My Own Story

Preparatory Meeting
This follows the same format, elements and time allocation as for the previous meeting.

1: Scripture/prayer/worship
John 20:19–31 is the assigned scripture reading. A volunteer reads it for reflection, prayer and worship. Encourage an atmosphere where people can respond and/or pray spontaneously as they wish. During this meeting, they may be more forthcoming with reflections and prayer than during previous meetings.

2: Information
As participants at this stage are normally quite comfortable being together in their groups, and even look forward to meeting their host and one another, there may be little need to offer guidelines. At the same time, it can be useful to remind hosts of some or all of the following:

- that their primary role is to welcome each participant and to act as mentors in encouraging them in their relationship to God;
- that the Spirit of God is with them as hosts and mentors and that he is equally at work in the life of each participant;
- to encourage prayer within their small group. It will

help if each host shares a brief moment's prayer before the discussion begins. Then, before the meeting ends, take a few minutes of reflection together, encouraging anyone who wishes to verbalise their prayer. A helpful thought here is that the timekeeper announces that three to four minutes remain. This will act as the cue to pray together.

Some of the following questions may help initiate or continue discussion.

- How are you since we last met? Did anything of interest happen?
- Are you finding the booklet helpful? Can you say in what way(s)?
- What is your response to the story you have just heard?
- Can you remember a time when someone confided his or her personal story to you? Can you recall your reaction?
- Did you ever listen to a story that carried values different from yours, but which led you to better understand the speaker because of his or her sincerity?

3: Arrival
The hosts go to their own group area and greet and welcome people as they arrive.

Welcome
The one who welcomes participants invites them to become aware of the presence of the Lord, and shares a personal story of his influence upon his or her life. This may emerge from an incident in life, the daily reflections, or the theme of the current meeting. The scripture is proclaimed, as in previous meetings, and is followed by a time of silence.

Resources for Presentation

This presentation follows a similar format to that of the previous meeting. The first section comprises a brief overview of the power of personal story, and is no longer than ten minutes. The second section, of up to fifteen minutes, communicates examples of 'seeing' and 'reading' a divine influence in the experiences of the speaker's life. Examples may be taken from a life-changing event that led to a new understanding of self, of other people and of life in terms of Jesus Christ and his providence and love. Examples may equally be taken from very 'ordinary' events in life where Christ is seen as companion and active guide.

The important thing here is that the speaker is authentic and speaks out of a relationship with Jesus that is part of the landscape of his or her thinking and lifestyle. It is also important to speak with concrete images about the presence and influence of God in the examples presented. A striking way of making this presentation is to speak about a particular (time of) struggle when he or she came to sense and recognise the love and provision of God. This is not to suggest that this solved all questionings and difficulties but, rather, that it gave birth to a deeper trust. Another important factor in telling one's story is the background and spirituality of the audience, so employ images that best speak to them. The following reflections and stories may assist you in your reflection as you prepare a presentation, or as you guide another in his or her reflection and preparation.

The scripture of the meeting (Jn 20:19–31) is a good resource during this presentation. No doubt the disciples, including Thomas, never forgot what happened. Most likely, they were never the same again and lived with new trust and confidence in the plan of Jesus for their lives. They certainly had a new story to tell about his intervention in their experience. They could never deny that this actually happened. Imagine the enthusiasm with which they would have spoken about it. They would have had little difficulty describing what had happened. They had been afraid and disbelieving, then Jesus came. He spoke to them. They responded to him. They found new hope, courage and assurance in him.

This scripture carries another thought, which may be worth developing. Jesus takes account of the unique difficulties of the disciples and accordingly relates to them. To people who were deep in fear for their safety because the one they followed now lay in death, he says simply, 'Peace be with you'. He goes on to show them the imprint of the nails in his hands and side. Sensing their dread, he again assures them, 'Peace be with you'.

Jesus comes to Thomas. He treats him with total respect. He listens to his questions and doubts. He knows the cold rational stance he had professed, that he would only believe in Jesus if he saw definite signs that he was alive. Jesus is sensitive to his unique stance and personality and begins to speak. He invites him to place his hand in his side and touch the holes in his hands. Thomas no longer needs 'proof'. In this story we see that Jesus is not deterred by our doubts and questioning but relates to us in a way that respects us.

This scripture reminds us that Jesus loves. He still comes. He still wishes to treat us, and speak to us, according to our own uniqueness and personal situations. Each of us is a continuing story of his love and wisdom. However, we easily take this for granted. We can even forget it and think that we are our own creating. Our gathering, and time together here, helps us to become aware of his work in us.

John Locke (1642–1704)

John Locke, an English philosopher and social contract theorist, articulated thinking about the importance of having some form of a civic public forum in place. For him, government would be good only if it received the consent of the governed and protected the natural rights to life, liberty and estate. Essentially, a civic public forum seeks to achieve this and questions how the various strands of values and thinking of a people can be heard and accommodated. It thus asks how, at the level of public policy and the legal and political systems as well as that of the informal and voluntary debates, speeches and discussions, the voices of both religious and non-religious natures can be heard for the betterment of society by those who govern.[84]

In our pluralist post-modern society, when scientific and rational certainties have yielded to a more subjective existential understanding of truth, there exist great opportunities to share the Christian narrative in daily conversations. When every story has an equal merit as the personal experience of one or more people, then it can equally lay claim that every story is equally to be heard. Today, Christian believers know that, culturally, they can no longer claim to be the only people with truth. They realise that they exist as living one set of convictions and experiences among many. In this spirit, they are called upon to know their story, and their deepest truth, and to share it as their experience towards the good of society and people. They can expect to be questioned about its truth, its applicability to real-life situations, and its authenticity. When they shy away from so sharing it, faith becomes endangered as an influence in the public forum, and reduced to a private comfort for its adherents.

St Teresa of Ávila (1515–1582)

St Teresa of Ávila advised, 'Do not pray for lighter burdens; pray for stronger backs.' Her advice is applicable to the disciples. In the scripture reading above, we see, for example, how Jesus comforted the disciples and touched them with his peace and the assurance of his presence during a difficult time. In this way, he was also preparing them for mission in the years ahead when they would face persecution and trial, and would need 'stronger backs'.

St Teresa's advice can prompt participants to recognise that Jesus had given them 'stronger backs' during a time of struggle when they may have hoped that their difficulty would have evaporated and be taken away from them. Her insight can help them interpret or re-interpret aspects of their stories in terms of God's goodness.

---

84 I see connections between John Locke's thinking and the outline of work for the Citizens' Assembly in Ireland. The challenge is that the Assembly be representative of people's values and perspectives.

I remember a moment about fifteen years ago when I experienced a great sense of personal freedom. For much of my life, I had lived with self-imposed difficulties. I considered I had a deep faith in God and was thankful that I trusted his providence. At the same time, I thought I had to be continuously 'proving' to myself that he exists. This, I believe, came from my need for certainty. Perhaps it also came from my ambition to have clear understanding and arguments so that I could convince another to come to believe in God. There was perhaps a more fundamental reason why I thought like this, namely a suspicion that God was a somewhat distant figure whom I could fully contact only by reason, and that other people would come to belief only when they had clear rational arguments.

Gradually, I came to name my own experience, and to trust the truth of my intuitions and faith in God. This helped me live with a new sense of freedom. Yes, my experience was different from that of other people, but it was mine. I could not doubt it. Yes, it was limited as my story and I conceded that perhaps it carried some false emphases. However, I could not deny that this was my unique experience. Ultimately, I realised that I can only know what my experience and story tell me. This gave me great confidence to trust it, while remaining aware of its limitations. It also gave me a greater readiness to share it with other people as my story and insight into life. This was not complacency or arrogance on my part, but peace in sharing my story, respect and tolerance in listening to other stories, and an openness to grow in understanding of my own story.

From all eternity God has thought of us and has loved us as unique individuals. He has called every one of us by name as the Good Shepherd 'calls his own sheep by name' (Jn 10:3). However, only in the unfolding of the history of our lives and its events is the eternal plan of God revealed to each of us. Therefore, it is a gradual process; in a certain sense, it is a process that happens day by day.[85]

Research by a father and son undertaken among young adults

85   *CL*, 58.

from largely Pentecostal Churches throughout the US found a rapid dropout rate of 70 per cent from church participation between 16–20 years of age.[86] Their conclusion is that adults and parents had failed to disciple their children,[87] who had in reality never been believers in the first place. They found that the leading factor for such a high dropout rate was that, while parents attended church, they had not shared with their children their personal reasons for doing so, and had never told them the story of their own personal faith journey. They concluded that for this reason children grew up with the impression that the Church and its services were empty rituals, devoid of personal significance.[88]

John Newton (1725–1807)

John Newton was born in London. Through the influence of his mother, he grew up in the Anglican Church. As a little boy he went to church and learned scripture stories and teachings from his mother. After her death, when he was only six years of age, he lived with his stepmother. Then, at the age of eleven, he began to travel with his father, who was the captain and owner of a cargo ship. The 'cargo' often comprised 200–300 African slaves, crowded together, lying next to one another, in the ship's hold.

During a big storm, John Newton was washed overboard but was soon picked up on the open seas by a slave trader who began to train him in the cargo trade. Gradually he began to be known for his irreverence, immorality, profanity and disrespect for all authority. He not only neglected his faith but also directly opposed it, while deriding others who practised it and denouncing God as a myth.

In 1748, on a return voyage to England, Newton was caught in a terrible storm off the coast of Donegal. All who were aboard the *Greyhound* thought they would soon drown. The scriptures and the

---

86   Rainer S. Thom and Sam S. Thom, *Essential Church? Reclaiming a Generation of Dropouts*, Nashville, TN: Publishing Group, 2008.
87   Ibid., 30.
88   Ibid., 97–101.

prayers John had once learned at his mother's knee came to his mind, and he became deeply aware that he was a dreadful sinner. He began to cry out to Jesus for mercy and to save him. For the first time in years, John prayed to God and, as he later wrote, 'the Lord sent from on high and delivered me out of deep waters.'

Newton had begun to realise the enormity of evil in his life and his complicity in the evil of slavery and slave trading. He turned from drinking, gambling and profanity. He had come to a time of change. The date was 10 May 1748. For the rest of his life, he marked this date each year as the anniversary of his conversion. About two weeks later, the greatly battered *Greyhound*, with its starving crew, arrived at Lough Swilly and safety.

Some time later, Newton left the ship and began to study Christian theology. He was ordained a minister of the Church of England in 1764 and became a zealous pastor. Thanking God for the grace of conversion, and to illustrate his sermon on New Year's Day in 1773, he composed a song that is now one of our favourite hymns: 'Amazing Grace, how sweet the sound, that saved a wretch like me. I once was lost but now am found, was blind but now I see.' Here was his spiritual autobiography in verse.

Before Departure

After the group discussions, before people depart, bring the following issues to the attention of participants.

- Remind them that each person has his or her own unique experience of life and values; each has a story to tell and each has a book that they could write.
- Outline a process to help them determine and/or deepen the experience of their story of faith. The following material can help you greatly. You may decide to print a copy of it for each person.

Writing One's Faith Story

Take a large page. Draw a line, divided into sections, each representing ten years. Mark in important people and events along that line. Reflect upon the significance of each person and event.

Notice the person or event that carries the greatest significance for you in so far as it initiates or deepens your relationship with the Lord. Describe it in writing. The following questions may focus your recollections and its continuing impact upon the way you live.

- Describe what you were like before this event.
  - What were your attitudes, values, questions, difficulties?
  - What engaged your time and your thinking?
  - Where were you seeking contentment and security?

- Describe why this event is so significant.
  - What factors led to this being a deeper step towards Jesus?
  - How did you react when you were faced with a decision for him?
  - What did the precise moment of surrender feel like for you?

- Describe the changes you now notice as a result.
  - What area(s) have changed for you since that time? (Be clear that this does not suggest perfection or point of arrival.)

Finally, speak about the next meeting, which will provide participants and hosts with an opportunity to renew their baptismal promises. At its core, it will be a reflective and moving ritual, which makes explicit the decision to live as missionary disciples of Jesus and be led by the movement of his Spirit. This is the central meeting of the programme, and always, in my experience, engenders a serene and joyful celebratory atmosphere. Encourage everyone to look forward to their next meeting, and to surround the coming week with a sense of occasion, prayer, preparation and reflection.

The meeting ends with the usual formula.

Fifth Meeting

Renewal of Baptism

The Layout of the Room

A change of ambience will communicate a sense of occasion to participants as they arrive. The guiding intention is to shape the room so that it is a place of welcome, conducive to relaxed reflection and prayer. Subdued lighting, achieved by placing candles and/or lights, for example, table lamps, strategically around the room, can assist greatly.

A centrepiece, as a point of focus, communicates a sense of sacred space. This is easily achieved with a multicoloured cloth or a number of different textiles, extending over different levels as objects of various heights are placed on the floor underneath it. A copy of the scriptures, together with a candle, is placed on this centrepiece. Flowers may also be placed on it, or positioned nearby. The paschal candle is given a place of prominence as a reminder of the light and life that comes to us from Christ.

You will already have decided whether there will be one or more locations to which participants can come as they renew their promises and pray for the grace of discipleship. The number of people in attendance will serve as your guide, as well as the time each participant is likely to take, and is given, to declare their intentions and in prayer. Your decision determines the number of tables or raised places you need. Drape a cloth over each, and place a bowl of water on the cloth. I suggest that the water is already blessed earlier that day during a public mass. This links the ritual being undertaken with the Eucharist, the parish, its ceremonies and its people. The actual process as people come forward is explained more fully during the ritual below.

Candles should also be available and one should be handed to each participant towards the end of the ritual. Each candle may carry the printed name of an individual. This possibility will depend on the regularity of attendance and on the system of obtaining names. Where it is not clear who is likely to attend, it may be best simply to call out each person's Christian name and give them a candle that is not personalised.

I have simply suggested a few guidelines to enhance the ambience of the room in keeping with the spirit of the event and its ritual. My best suggestion is that you involve a number of creative people to carry out this task.

Preparatory Meeting
This follows the same format, elements and time allotment as previous meetings.

1:Scripture/prayer/worship
John 9:1–17; 24–25; 35–38 is the scripture reading to prompt reflection, prayer and worship. Encourage personal responses spontaneous prayer, which may include intercessions for each participant and invoking the Holy Spirit.

2: Information
Give an overview of meeting. It follows the pattern of previous meetings – welcome and presentation. The ritual of baptismal renewal will follow. Of particular interest to hosts will be to know what is expected of them. Essentially, their role is to accompany each participant in their group as she or he comes forward to the blessed water. This movement symbolises the desire to be followers and disciples of Jesus. It is a moment of decision. Participants are

accompanied by the host(s) of their group. This expresses the prayer and support of the community for the person who is undertaking a new decision for Christ. What is more important is to communicate attitudes beyond what they are to do. These include:

- Surrender of oneself to God, knowing that his loving plan is more than what they desire and far greater than they can achieve by their own efforts;
- Trust in God's Spirit and in his promises that if anyone is thirsty, comes to him, and believes in him, from their heart 'shall flow rivers of living water' (Jn 7:37–38);
- Awareness of each individual in the group;
- Prayer that each will have the grace of surrender to Jesus or at least of openness to his love.

At the end of this preparatory meeting, hosts go as usual to their group area and welcome and greet people as they arrive. However, there will be no group discussion and no questions. This meeting is primarily a prayer experience. Music enhances it to such an extent that it is a necessity. However, it is important that the music and hymns chosen lead to worship of God, while people may join in or remain in quiet reflection.

3: Welcome

The continuity person informally communicates a public welcome to all. She or he introduces the general format and theme for the meeting. A personal incident or story attunes its significance to real-life situations for participants. On one occasion, as part of the welcome, I heard a story about the graceful and effortless movement of a young girl on a skateboard who seemed 'to float not by might, and not by power'. The speaker went on to tell about her efforts to be good and the demands she placed on herself to live up to her Christian standards in her earlier years. While these standards remain important to her, she noticed that many times life for her became like 'floating with the Holy Spirit' after she had turned to Christ to follow him. The impact of this story was that it provided a moment's review and helped those listening to relax, to trust in the goodness of God and to be open to the influence of the Holy Spirit.

A hymn of worship can now help deepen the sense of God's goodness and of the dynamic presence and power of his Spirit. The reading from scripture follows. A period of reflection provides a fruitful space, as does the option of two to four people sharing a phrase, a word or a very brief insight, as their spontaneous response to what they heard in the scripture.

Resources for Presentation
Drawing attention to a few different features, for example the subdued lighting, can serve as a good reminder to participants of the uniqueness of this occasion. It can also initiate and help establish a positive contact with them.

Drawing attention to an aspect of the scriptures proclaimed can serve to link a very rich story with the meaning of the evening's event. Here is an example of one I used when making this presentation. Some neighbours asked the blind man: 'Then how were your eyes opened?' (Jn 9:10). He told them all he knew. He spoke of a man called Jesus (v. 11). He did as the man told him, namely, to wash in the pool at Siloam, and then he regained his sight. He told them that he did not know the present whereabouts of the man. Evidently, he saw Jesus as merely human and not as Lord and Messiah. Neither did he know why Jesus approached him. All he knew for certain was that he had been blind and now he could see. He did not understand its full significance. It remained somewhat of a puzzle for him. Now he saw with his physical eye. Later, he would come face to face with Jesus. He would regain a new sight and 'see' Jesus as the Lord (v. 38), the one who was sent from the Father to bring sight to the blind.

This is also a mysterious moment for each of us. We may not fully understand why we are attending this programme. All we know is that we saw a notice, met someone who told us about it, read about it in a local paper, or heard someone speak about it on radio or from the pulpit. And now here we are. Perhaps, neither do we fully grasp what – or, more properly, who – is being offered to us. All we know is that for some reason we did arrive here; that something seems to be changing for us; and we wish to explore further the attraction and changes that are happening for us. We also sense that here is a beginning for us, as we see the man or person called Jesus. May we, too, like the blind man, come to see him as prophet (v. 17) and acknowledge him as 'from God' (v. 33); and, finally, as Lord, when we will bow down and 'worship him' (v. 38). In a word, we, too, wish to make our own personal journey from blindness to new sight, even though we may now fail to grasp what this means, or where it may lead us.

This evening we are doing something dangerous. It is so easy to become a Catholic in Ireland today. Bring a child for baptism and that person then remains a Catholic unless she or he formally and officially revokes it. It was not always like this. At many times during the Church's history, people who made a decision for Christ, and a decision to stand with the people of God, risked danger. For the first 300 years of the Church's life, for example, persecution was a distinct possibility.

At times, our 'enlightened' age is described as an age of persecution. You may wish to name places where today to live and profess Christian faith, or to carry a bible or a religious object, is dangerous and, in a number of isolated instances, means death. You may wish to name one or two current examples where a public acknowledgement of faith means suffering or even death. You may also wish to draw attention to a 'subtle' form of persecution that exists in the Western world, which, while it is not overtly persecutory, is embedded in facets of cultural life as negativity and hostility towards particular religious values and denominations. Again, you may wish to cite an example or two that you observe.

This evening we make a new decision as adults, and commit ourselves to following Christ. We desire to become his disciples and journey through various thresholds or stages of conversion, as did the blind man.

I like the word surrender. This ritual provides the opportunity to surrender to God and into the embrace of Jesus. It facilitates for participants the acceptance of Jesus' love for them, that they are heirs to the many promises he has made. You might consider drawing attention to one or two promises that Jesus made and that carry life and significance for you. I have already quoted one of his promises, namely, that as we thirst and come to him, and believe in him, then out of our 'heart shall flow rivers of living water' (Jn 7:37–38). He also promised that he would send the Holy Spirit 'he will guide you into all the truth' (Jn 16:13). Again, Jesus invites us to become his people and empowers us to go in service and mission towards all people, knowing that as we 'make disciples of the nations', we can rely on his promise, 'I am with you always, to the end of the age' (Mt 28:19–20).

In the gospel story of the blind man, we see the power of Jesus to change, to heal and to make a difference. It is in the name of the same Jesus that we gather. When we lose the sense of the power of Jesus, we lose the power of Christianity. It remains simply a structure, a legal system, a moral code, but without the expectation of the influence of a living God.

One of the difficulties we may have with the term 'renewal of our baptismal promises' is that many will likely remember undertaking such a renewal in the past. They may remember, for example, renewing their promises on Holy Saturday night or Easter morning or, indeed, being conscious of it each time they make the sign of the cross, which is sometimes referred to as a mini-baptism. Yet, either little or nothing may seem to have happened. They undertook it simply as part of the expected ritual of the day or almost as a reflex action, as in the case of the sign of the cross. It failed to carry any sense of newness, or any expectation of changed attitudinal or behavioural patterns. This now presents a challenge for the speaker in communicating a sense of the richness of baptism, and announce that its inner experience is now available to all. It is like being invited to cross a border into a new territory, which offers a new lifestyle and a new language.

To renew baptismal promises is to expect Christ to make a difference in the lives of people present. He wishes to release his Spirit, already received at their baptism but never accepted by them in a conscious way, with any great influence on their patterns of life. The experience of the early Church is also for us today: 'having received from the Father the promise of the Holy Spirit, he has poured out this that you both see and hear' (Acts 2:33). This is equally true for us here and now. Do you remember the story about when people brought the sick and the infirm and laid them along the side of the street so that the shadow of Peter might fall upon them? This story can inspire participants to have a similar expectancy of faith. The story of the blind man can also be re-entered and become each person's story. It can point to how they can expect God's grace to be active and real for them as they yield to him in self-surrender.

Imagine the vibrancy of the blind man. Imagine his sense of joy, wonder and discovery. He was healed of his blindness. He had received what he had been looking for – his sight. We, too, live with blindness. We don't see God as he is. He is described, for example, as 'a devouring fire' of love. We read, 'since we are receiving a kingdom that cannot be shaken, let us give thanks, by which we offer to God an acceptable worship with reverence and awe; for indeed our God is a consuming fire' (Heb 12:28–29).[89]

Pope Francis urges us not to 'cage the Spirit of God'. In this way, he invites us to set free the Spirit of God within who desires to guide us into personal freedom from all that holds us caged, addicted and dominated. This image, when elaborated upon, can be very powerful in outlining the work that God wishes to achieve in the heart and spirit of each person.

---

89   See also Deuteronomy 4:24 and Isaiah 33:14, even though the emphasis there is more on God's judgement.

It is equally true that we don't see ourselves as we are, as sinners in need, yet children of God, totally loved by him. Thomas Merton, describing his deepest identity, said, 'I am one who is loved by God'. Antonio Spadaro SJ, interviewed Pope Francis while preparing an article for *La Civiltà Cattolica*.[90] One of his questions to him was simply, 'Who is Jorge Mario Bergoglio? 'I am a sinner,' the pope replied. This is a most accurate definition. It is not a figure of speech, a literary genre. I am a sinner. Here, this is me, a sinner on whom the Lord has turned his gaze ... I am a sinner, but I trust in the infinite mercy and patience of our Lord Jesus Christ.

Nor do we see others as they are. We can so easily see their faults, rather than their divine-bearing dignity. I can recall Desmond Forristal saying, 'Were we to stand before a congregation of people and see them as they are we would need dark glasses to prevent being blinded by the radiance and the light of Christ before us.'[91]

Baptism is the door of entry into the community of Christian faith. It immerses us in the reality of community life. It opens us to give and receive within the networks of our relationships. Baptism makes us members of the Body of Christ: 'for we are members of one another' (Ep 4:25). Baptism incorporates us into the Church. From the baptismal fonts is born the one people of God of the New Covenant, which transcends all the natural and human limits of nations, cultures, races and sexes: 'For in the one Spirit we were all baptised into one body' (1 Cor 12:13).[92]

The man cured of blindness spoke about the difference Jesus made in his life. He had a story to tell. He had good news to share. He did not understand it, but he wished to tell it to encourage other people to come to the source of good news. He simply said: 'All I know is that once I was blind; now I see.' For Paul VI, one of the obstacles to

90   Spadaro, editor-in-chief of the Italian Jesuit journal, *La Civiltà Cattolica*, interviewed Pope Francis in August 2013. The eighteen-page in-depth interview was also published in *L'Osservatore Romano*, 21 September 2013.
91   Desmond Forristal (1930–2012) was a priest, broadcaster, playwright and documentary maker. He lived what he professed, with great appreciation of the dignity of each person he met.
92   *CCC*, 1267.

evangelisation is the 'apathy and especially the lack of joy and hope in many of our evangelisers'.[93] The man who had just regained his sight had known the power of Jesus to make a difference. He was happy to talk about what he had experienced and to answer simply the questions he was asked. Here is a beautiful story of what God can do, and of sharing faith (evangelising). For John Paul II, 'an evangelist is a witness to the experience of Christ'.[94]

The blind man was not just passive in his healing. He had a part to play. He knew he was blind. He did something about it. He allowed Jesus to draw near. Then he went and washed in the waters of Siloam. The truth is that we, too, have a part to play in committing ourselves to Christ and to his transforming power. However, we may not wish to change. We may be too afraid to let go of our sin, our selfishness, our resentments and hurts, because we fear our ability to cope in a new situation. You may be able to draw upon example(s) of a person or set of people who continued to live in intolerable circumstances because for them it had become normal, and they did not want the uncertainty of life in different circumstances.

The truth is that change is possible. You may recall the story of the man who for thirty-eight years had waited at the Sheep Pool in Jerusalem for the water to be disturbed, but he was never the first to go into it because he needed help and it was not available to him (Jn 5:1–9). He could easily have become disillusioned, cold and fatalistic and yield up any hope of ever being healed. Yet, this does not seem to have happened. He seemed to have retained some hope that one day he would be first into the water. Otherwise, why did he continue to wait?

All that is expected of us is to allow ourselves to be drawn closer to Christ and to trust that he wishes to do the most loving thing in our lives. Our task is to give him permission to do in and through us what he desires to do.

93   EN, 79.
94   John Paul II, Address to Third General Conference of the Latin American Episcopate, Puebla, Mexico, 28 January 1979.

The paschal theme can equally be greatly beneficial in leading to the heart of baptismal renewal in that it carries the dynamics of dying and rising in Christ, and then in human experience and in nature. Joseph Ratzinger understands the death of Jesus as an act of hope. His 'death, which by its nature is the end, the destruction of every relationship, is by him transformed into an act of communication of himself; and this is the salvation of humankind, in that it signifies that love conquers death'.[95] For John Paul II, the cycle of the paschal mystery is the 'masterpiece' of the Holy Spirit. He further explains, 'the newness of God is already found in Jesus' Pasch. It is this which brings the Church to birth, inspires her life, and renews and transforms her history'.[96] You may wish to elaborate further on his thinking. A fruitful way of giving it reality may be through reference to examples where you know the transforming power of God is at work. Such examples, whether from your personal experiences, or heard from people you know, centre on experiences of loss, inferiority, hurt or injustice, to become a source of gift and of inspiration in ministry to people similarly limited or wounded. They describe a journey where situations of dying have yielded to situations of new life.

St Gregory Nazianzus tells us that 'Baptism is God's most beautiful and magnificent gift … We call it gift, grace, anointing, enlightenment, garment of immortality, bath of rebirth, seal and most precious gift. It is called gift because it is conferred on those who bring nothing of their own; grace since it is given even to the guilty; baptism because sin is buried in the water; anointing for it is priestly and royal as are those who are anointed; enlightenment because it radiates light; clothing since it veils our shame; bath because it washes; and seal as it is our guard and the sign of God's Lordship.'[97]

It is clear that the speaker can explore many lines of thinking. Indeed, there are other useful themes for exploration, for example

95 Joseph Ratzinger, *Il cammino pasquale*, Milan: Ancora, 1985, cited by Aidan Nichols in *The Thought of Benedict XVI*, London: Burns & Oates, 2007, 146.
96 Pope John Paul II, *Ecclesia in Europa*, 106.
97 St Gregory Nazianzus, Oration 40, 3–4, 36, 361C.

baptism as a basis of pastoral community and of ministry. However, it is important to stress that ten to fifteen minutes is the optimum time for this presentation, and that its primary intention is to inspire and lead participants to entrust themselves to Christ, who heals blindness and wishes to immerse all in the experience of his light and life.

Ritual of the Renewal of Baptism

Most fundamentally, the renewal of baptismal promises here brings to awareness the experience that is at the heart of baptism. It also serves to root the programme in the Christian tradition. Perhaps, for this reason it helps when someone associated with leadership in the parish or the community leads the ceremony, as it signifies that the commitments being undertaken are within and for the life of the parish and Church. The actual ceremony of baptism is closely followed, taking account of this particular setting. Through listening to the words, we hear again what is our reality and heritage through our baptism, and are awakened to experience it now as our adult decision. A hymn brings the presentation to a conclusion.

Participants are then prepared for their renewal of baptism through prayers for repentance and healing. They may be invited to remain silent for a few moments and may wish to close their eyes during the time of guided prayer.

Guided prayer

You may invite another person to lead this or undertake it yourself.

Our Need for Repentance

Lord Jesus, we want to be people of truth. We want to be people who live in the light. We now repent of our sin. We know you are present to us as the one who forgives us. We turn our lives completely over to you. We accept you as our Lord and Saviour. We thank you for welcoming us into your love and that your forgiveness is real. Your mercy is new each day and we thank you for now clothing us once again as a new creation. We make our prayer through you, the Christ, the Son of the living God. Amen.

Our Need for Healing
Jesus came, too, to heal the wounds of sin and division.

LORD, you have said: 'I have come that they might have life, and have it abundantly' (Jn 10:10). Lord, we ask your Holy Spirit to walk with us to the places of darkness in our lives. We live in a world of sin and division, where people hurt and are hurting. We pray that you take us to an event, which has deeply distressed us and which we think still holds us captive.

LORD, I enter into that time of distress. I feel again the sense of being alone, the confusion, the sense of no one being there to help me. I feel again all the emotions that may have surrounded it: rejection, the guilt of thinking that it was my own fault, the futility of life as I looked into the future. Lord, I stay here for a short time, reliving again this time of darkness.

LORD, I now look to you. That moment is now present to you. I see you walking into that time in my life. What are your eyes of love and compassion telling me? Your hands reaching out to me: What are my thoughts? I see your smile, as if you wish to bless me ... I hear your whisper: What are your words that you are speaking in my ear?

LORD, I know you can free me from being held captive by the anger, the fear, the inferiority before others and the resentment that is still part of me from that time.

Lord, I know that 'all things work together for good for those who love God' (Rom 8:28). Lord, I present all the painful situations of my life to you ... the addictions ... the times of fear ... the times I felt betrayed and crushed ... I pray that the experience of my weakness and brokenness will lead not to despair but to new trust in your goodness. I pray too that through knowing my own poverty you will lead me to a deeper understanding and compassion towards all who are in need.

Lord, I thank you for all my life, for all that I may describe as good and for all that I may describe as bad. It has all led me to this moment, when I give my life to you as the one who heals and forgives. Fill me now with a deep love for you and for all whom I meet each day.

We make our prayer through you, the Christ, the Son of the living God. Amen.

There are many prayers available for inner healing, which you may find useful here. You may equally wish to abridge the prayer for healing by, for example, deciding to delete the first four paragraphs.

Welcome
The Christian community again welcomes you with great joy. In its name you were claimed for Christ our Saviour by the sign of the cross.

Each person makes the sign of the cross on his or her forehead by way of association with that moment when it was made at their baptism by parents and godparents.

Prayer of Exorcism and Anointing
We take the authority of Christ over all evil.

Almighty and ever-living God, you sent your only Son into the world to cast out the power of Satan, spirit of evil, to rescue your people from the kingdom of darkness, and bring them into the splendour of your kingdom of light. The prayer at our baptism was for you to set us free from original sin, to make us temples of your glory, and to send your Holy Spirit to dwell within us. We were anointed with the oil of salvation in the name of Christ our Saviour to strengthen us with his power, who lives and reigns for ever and ever. Amen.

Profession of Faith
A profession of faith is part of preparation for baptism. In the event of children's baptism, adults profess their faith to express their decision to commit to following Jesus. It is also their declaration that they want an environment of faith, hope and love for the happy and Christian maturing of their children. During the *Rite of Christian Initiation of Adults*, the Apostles' Creed is clearly explained to the catechumenates, and then, following the first scrutiny during the fifth week of Lent, each is presented with a copy of the Creed.

This evening you may simply lead people in reciting the Apostles' Creed. Alternatively, you may invite their response to a series of questions that you deem best express their commitment. I now include the wording from the Rite of Baptism.

Rite of Baptism
You have come here to renew the promises made for you at your baptism. By water and the Holy Spirit you then received the gift of new life from God, who is love.

On your part, you must make it your constant care to continue in the practice of the faith. See that the divine life, which God gives you, is kept safe from the poison of sin, to grow always stronger in your hearts.

If your faith makes your ready to accept this responsibility, renew now the vows of your baptism. Reject sin; profess your faith in Christ Jesus. This is the faith of the Church.

Do you reject Satan?
All: I do.
And all his works?
All: I do.
And all his empty promises?
All: I do.
Do you believe in God, the Father almighty, creator of heaven and earth?
All: I do.
Do you believe in Jesus Christ, his only Son, our Lord, who was born of the Virgin Mary, was crucified, died and was buried, rose from the dead, and is now seated at the right hand of the Father?
All: I do.
Do you believe in the Holy Spirit, the holy Catholic Church, the communion of saints, the forgiveness of sins, the resurrection of the body and life everlasting?
All: I do.
This is our faith. This is the faith of the Church. We are proud to profess it in Christ Jesus our Lord.
All: Amen.

Ritual of Renewal
Participants, as they feel ready, now come forward to the blessed water. Each pauses for a moment in silent reflection. They then make

the sign of the cross on their foreheads with the water. This serves as a link with their baptism. It is also a gesture of their commitment to Christ and of their 'yes' to appropriating their baptism.

Their host accompanies each, stands behind them, and places a hand on their shoulder immediately before they trace the sign of the cross. This reminds them of the support of the community as they commit to living a more ardent faith. In the early days of the Church this gesture was part of the prayer of the community for the outpouring of the Holy Spirit on those seeking a deeper faith.

The leader greets them as they stand in front of the bowl of water. She or he may ask each participant, 'What do you want us to pray for you?' After the sign of the cross the leader places a hand on the participant's head. The prayer may be very simple, for example, 'May the Lord meet the desires of your heart'. When time allows, there may be a longer time of prayer, while host(s) may also verbalise a prayer for each. Meanwhile, everyone else is in prayer, in particular for one another, as they move forward publicly declaring for Christ and renewing their faith. Hymn singing and music provide a wonderful backdrop to prayer.

After everyone has returned to their places the following from the rite of baptism is said. A brief reference to these words with their accompanying symbols help to bring out their significance for participants.

God the Father of our Lord Jesus Christ has freed you from sin, given you a new birth by water and the Holy Spirit, and welcomed you into his holy people. At your baptism he anointed you with the chrism of salvation. As Christ was anointed Priest, Prophet, and King, so may you live always as a member of his body sharing everlasting life.
All: Amen.

You have become a new creation and have clothed yourself in Christ. At baptism you were clothed in a white garment as the outward sign of your Christian dignity. With your family, friends and the community to help you by word and example, now continue to bring that dignity unstained into the everlasting life of heaven.

All: Amen.

Each person comes forward on hearing their name called out, announcing: 'N, Receive, the light of Christ'. A small candle, lit from the paschal candle, is then presented to each person. When everyone has received their candle, the leader prays the following words:

These lights are entrusted to you to be kept burning brightly. You have been enlightened by Christ. You are to walk always as a child of the light. May you keep the flame of faith alive in your hearts. When the Lord comes, may you go out to meet him with all the saints in the heavenly kingdom.

The Lord Jesus made the deaf hear and the dumb speak. May he continue to touch your ears to receive his word, and your mouth to proclaim his faith, to the praise and glory of God the Father.

All: Amen.

Final Prayer

By God's gift, through water and the Holy Spirit, we are reborn to everlasting life. In his goodness, may he continue to pour out his blessings upon us, who are his sons and daughters. May he make us always wherever we may be faithful members of his holy people. May he send his peace upon all who are gathered here in Christ our Lord.

All: Amen.

*All stand and sing a suitable hymn or two, for example 'This Little
Light of Mine', 'The Light of Christ', 'Go Tell Everyone'. Each person
holds a lighted candle. There is a great sense of joy and hope as people look
outwards to the world to bring the light of Christ.*

Departure

Candles are carefully extinguished. Participants are informed of
a change in format during the next meeting, which will conclude
the programme. It will begin as usual with welcome, scripture,
presentation and testimony. Group discussions will follow. The
meeting will look at where and how people can find support in living
out their faith joyfully and with conviction, with particular reference
to the support and encouragement a small faith community can give.
The evening will end with a simple celebration to which people may
wish to bring something to eat or drink.

End with offering all present a word of encouragement. They are
indeed the Light of Christ for others.

Sixth Meeting

God's Surprises

Be careful, if the Church is alive, she must always surprise. To surprise is typical of the living Church. A Church that no longer has the capacity to surprise is a weak, sick and dying Church that must be brought into the emergency room and resuscitated as soon as possible. (Pope Francis)[98]

Preparatory Meeting
This follows the same format, elements and time allotted as previously. Acts 2:42–47 is the assigned scripture reading. Here we witness the surprises of God at work, as we hear about the foundations and growth of the early body of disciples. You can expect a greater quality of participation, reflection, praise and spontaneous prayer. Encourage brief feedback about the previous meeting and give an outline of this final one.

Questions
The following questions may prompt discussion among the participants:
  • How are you since last week? How did you find the booklet readings?
  • What did the scripture reading suggest to you?
  • What is your reaction to the presentation you heard?
  • Have you thought about what happens next for you?
  • Do you have any questions?

98   Pope Francis, St Peter's Square, Pentecost Sunday, 8 June 2104, before praying the Regina Coeli.

Welcome
The hosts go to their group area and greet people as they arrive. The continuity person welcomes everyone warmly, enquires about the experiences of the previous week, and offers a reflection that is relevant to this week's meeting. Scripture is then proclaimed and reflected upon.

Resources for Presentation
I have found that a striking way of making this presentation is by sketching a vision of God's call for the Christian person (and of Church/parish) in contemporary culture. You can select from the quotes and images below. You will also have your own images and resources upon which to draw.

Evangelisation is the context of this presentation. It explores how participation in a small faith community can benefit and nurture individuals to take on a spirit of evangelisation and mission towards others, especially through their words of faith and encouragement. The story about Maximilian Kolbe (see page 81) may serve to bridge the themes of this meeting and of previous meetings.

The first section of this presentation examines the principles that underpin community, which supports Christian living and the task of evangelisation. The second conveys, in story form, the personal benefits of such a community in living out one's faith. A different person may present each section.

In a world where there is loneliness, selfishness, addiction, poverty, fear, injustice and conflict, the word of God in scripture and Church teaching reveals to us the broad direction we are to take. It can be summed up as loving God and our neighbour. It can equally be summed up as 'Come to me; and go out to the whole world.'

Recognising that some people may already have made decisions about what they plan to do after these six weeks demonstrates confidence in participants and respects their freedom. Some, for example, may have decided to set aside time for personal prayer, to read and listen to the Word of God, to undertake a programme of study or an initiative or activity on behalf of the poor.

At the same time, the core of this presentation is community as a fundamental facet of faith, and how its dynamics of giving and receiving, of sharing faith and looking outwards towards all people, supports Christian living. It is also helpful to reflect back to participants if the idea of parish cells has surfaced from among them as a likely follow-up. Some reflections about small faith communities follow. The intention is that this presentation, in selecting a number of them, and drawing upon other resources, will provide information for informed decisions. 'Where two or three meet in my name, I am there with them' (Mt 18:20).

In Acts 2:42–47 we see the practices of the early followers of Jesus as they devoted themselves to the teaching of the apostles, fellowship, breaking of bread and prayers. They lived community life through temple meetings, gatherings in the home and attentiveness to those in need among them. These practices continued for the first 300 years of Church history.

Pope Francis speaks about a 'culture of encounter' as a central element in Church life. Its importance arises because it continues the pastoral style of Jesus, who came to serve and not to be served. His interest was the human person and encountering each person in their reality and poverty, even when it takes them to the peripheries of loneliness, sin, fear and failure. Jesus identifies with them and, no matter what their circumstances, meets them as people with the dignity of being made in God's image. This, too, is to be the Christian way for all who profess to follow him. For Francis a culture of encounter leads people beyond the diversity of ideologies and religion to community and the unity of all people. He sees that it also provides adequate answers to the problem of hunger, and to the problems that affect the dignity of every human being. The Church cannot be merely a babysitter who takes care of the child just to get him to sleep. That would make her a slumbering Church.[99]

99   Pope Francis addressed these themes on a number of occasions, for example, 22 May 2013 and 16 October 2013.

A theme that is worth developing is the relationship of New Evangelisation and small faith communities where there exists newness about the way people live out Christianity and how they reach out to share it with other people.

'Apostolic movements appear in ever new forms in history … necessarily so, because they are the Holy Spirit's answer to the ever-changing situation in which the Church exists.'[100] The then Cardinal Joseph Ratzinger saw new ecclesial movements as surprises of God's Spirit.

An interesting study, for our context, would be to examine how, in Irish history, the faith of the people remained Catholic even though they remained under foreign rule with a different official denomination. Historian Patrick Corish suggested that this was largely due to the organisation of Church and society in that it was based on the local community of extended family and tribe and served by visiting clergy.[101]

The parish is described as a family of families and a community of communities. In other words, the intention is that it be made up of small groups and communities of people who interact, know and support one another, as well as pray for and with each other. Participants encourage and form one another in their Christian faith, and are attentive to those most in need, whether materially, physically, emotionally, intellectually or spiritually. Small faith communities make Christianity human and break through the anonymity that is prevalent in contemporary society.

So that all parishes may be truly communities of Christians, local ecclesial authorities ought to foster a) participation of the lay faithful in pastoral responsibilities; b) small, basic or so-called 'living' communities, where the faithful can communicate the Word of God and express it in service and love to one another; these

---

100   Joseph Ratzinger, 'The Ecclesial Movements: A Theological Reflection on Their Place in the Church', World Congress of the Ecclesial Movements, Rome, 27–29 May 1998. See also his address, 'The Theological Locus of Ecclesial Movements', in *Communion: International Catholic Review*, 25, no. 3, 1998, 480–504.
101   Patrick J. Corish, *The Irish Catholic Experience*, Dublin: Gill & Macmillan, 1985.

communities are true expressions of ecclesial communion and centres of evangelisation, in communion with their pastors.[102]

A solitary Christian is not a Christian. (Tertullian)

Parishes need to restructure because parishes, as we now have them are ineffective.
(Arthur Baronowski, *Creating Small Church Communities*)

The Church of the future will be one built from below by basic communities. (Karl Rahner)

Those of us who know Jesus cannot but want to share the message and experience with others; that is what evangelisation is about ... Unless we make radically new inroads in terms of evangelisation, then there is the risk that ... we will be out of business. ... How can we in this Diocese establish 'basic Christian communities' in which faith is formed and lived, in which people pray and worship, in which the love of Jesus is practised and which reaches out to all?[103]

Small faith communities are growing in a rapid way in most parts of the world today, most notably South America, the Philippines and Africa. They are doing so with a great variety of emphases and *charism*s.

St Ignatius of Loyola (1491–1556) was a Spanish knight from a Basque noble family. After being seriously wounded in the Battle of Pamplona in 1521, he had a long recovery period during which he began to read whatever books and articles were available to him in Loyola. He gradually noticed that books of a romantic nature left

102 *CL*, 26.
103 Archbishop Diarmuid Martin, Address, 'Moving From Parish to Church': Parish Development and Renewal Meeting for the Fingal South East, Fingal South West and Howth Deaneries, Holy Cross, Clonliffe, Dublin, 20 May 2004.

him empty, dispirited and drifting. On the other hand, he noticed that reading spiritual material, for example, the life of Christ and the lives of the saints, filled him with goodness, generosity and heroism. He began to wonder what he should do next and which path to pursue. His experience led to his spiritual conversion and laid the foundation for his principles and exercises on the discernment of spirits, which continue to influence people today to yield to God's plan for their lives.

To live is to change, and to be perfect is to have changed often (John Henry Newman). At the same time change is never easy. It is normally felt as challenge because it involves facing into our fears and deep-seated patterns of thinking and behaving.

The 'door of faith' (Acts 14:27) is always open for us, ushering us into the life of communion with God and offering entry into his Church. It is possible to cross that threshold when the word of God is proclaimed and the heart allows itself to be shaped by a transforming grace. To enter through that door is to set out on a journey that lasts a lifetime.(Pope Benedict XVI)[104]

The Church as a whole and all her Pastors, like Christ, must set out to lead people out of the desert towards the place of life, towards friendship with the Son of God, towards the One who gives us life and live in abundance. (Pope Benedict XVI)[105]

The second part of this presentation comprises insights into the significance and benefits of participating in a small faith community in the experience of the speaker. While it necessarily gives information about an actual faith community, it is primarily personal,

104 Pope Benedict XVI, *Porta Fidei*, 1.
105 Ibid., 2.

and descriptive of concrete attitudes and events. The background and the general thrust of the programme described here in *Inspiring Faith Communities* has deep roots in the parish cell experience. It is therefore appropriate to invite one or more people who already participate in this experience to present at least the second section of this final meeting. They may speak of the history, purposes and personal influence of parish cells, and suggest how individuals may be involved in them. Further information on this experience is available in Chapter 5 of this book. At the same time, the great value of this programme is that it can serve many purposes. This section may be used to present and describe a very different form of faith support, or to launch a particular pastoral initiative.

Participants, in their small groupings, now begin to share personal responses to what they have heard and to their experience of the programme. Generally, they readily and spontaneously engage in conversation during this final meeting. Some of the questions, given above, may provide focus, while the central question revolves around how participants may best support what they have experienced. The discussion ends with time set aside to complete the brief questionnaire on page 126.

Programme Conclusion
The programme concludes by drawing attention to a number of follow-up possibilities.

Very often the leadership team will propose an additional meeting in order to consolidate the experience of the programme and give participants time to clarify their follow-up, and to discern the direction and surprises God has for them as individuals. It may include input on the significance of evangelisation, and how small faith groups may direct its processes and support those who participate. It may simply be a time of reflection and listening on the part of participants upon their experiences, as well as prayer for direction and courage. It may comprise the celebration of the Eucharist as communal thanksgiving.

The parish team and/or local bishop may be invited to hear, at first hand, the fruit of the experience, and may wish to respond and affirm the experience and call all to evangelise.

Another follow-up possibility is to announce the dates of the next *Inspiring Faith Communities* programme. It may be possible to outline for those present a sense of responsibility and mission by suggesting how they can help this programme through prayer, spreading the word, advertising, being part of the steering team and acting as hosts.

Express a genuine thank you to all who have contributed to this programme. Above all, declare your delight in observing the participants coming to enjoy it, and in opening up to the person of Christ. A good way to conclude may be to associate with the final tweet of Benedict XVI, just hours before his resignation became official: 'Thank you for your love and support. May you always experience the joy that comes from putting Christ at the centre of your lives.'

There now remains the reception, when participants share what each has brought and engage in informal conversations. The programme ends when hosts and service team members of the steering team meet for a final time of prayer and evaluation.

Parish cells are like a software computer programme that a parish takes and plugs into its life. It is not a spirituality, it is a system of pastoral ministry. It is neither good nor bad. It depends on the user. Its purpose is to provide for lay formation and make disciples. Its three great benefits are

    a) relationship with Christ;

    b) community;

    c) evangelisation.

It makes possible a new vision of parish as a place of formation and mission, and as a community of communities.

INSPIRING FAITH COMMUNITIES

Feedback Form

DETAILS *(for those interested in a small faith group)*

Name: _____

Contact Number: _____

Address: _____

_____

Email Address: _____

Whether home may be available: ☐ Yes ☐ No *(please tick)*

COMMENTS *(for all)*

What did you find most helpful?

_____

_____

_____

What does it now mean for you?

_____

_____

_____

Any other comment/suggestion:

_____

_____

_____

Conclusion

Inspiring Faith Communities
A Personal Reflection

There is no greater freedom than that of allowing oneself to be guided by the Holy Spirit, renouncing the attempt to plan and control everything to the last detail, and instead letting him enlighten, guide and direct us wherever he wills. The Holy Spirit knows well what is needed in every time and place. This is what it means to be mysteriously fruitful.[106]

IN 1978, I was appointed as parish curate in Bayside, Dublin 13. During my first weeks, my duties were assigned. I was to 'take charge of altar servers, ministers of the Eucharist, and boy scouts'. I would be chairperson of one school and chaplain to another. I would visit up to 700 homes. My fellow curate already had his assigned duties and would visit approximately the same number in the rest of the parish.[107] I would take my place in the rota for masses, confessions, baptisms, etc. It was precise. It was predictable. I knew what was expected of me. No seminars or debates were required. All that was needed was to determine the times of the various events and I could begin. I felt it was manageable.

I paint the above picture to highlight profound changes in parish/

---

106 *EG*, 280.
107 The two curates visited the homes of the parish on a routine basis. The parish priest did not have 'duties'. I assumed the reason was that he was too old. He was in his late sixties, and the practice was 'to leave the work to the younger men'. This also points to the profound changes in pastoral personnel when we look today at the average age of Irish clergy in our parishes.

Church life in Ireland during the last forty years. Many of these are well documented, widely recognised and often deeply felt. I do not detail them here. Suffice to say that the Church has moved from a seemingly confident institution to one at the fringe of public discourse, and which now carries, in the perspective of many, signals of its collapse and irrelevance. Meanwhile, people have moved from reliance on the external authority of the Church to the primacy of their internal experience and intuitions. Emphasis on personal faith, transition, fluidity, uncertainty and searching tend to replace stability, confidence and predictability. The painful struggle within the Church in relation to facing up to the horrors of clerical child sex abuse and listening to the voices of victims, difficulties in working towards safeguarding and healing, together with the reality of debilitating clericalism, authoritarianism and mismanagement, provided the impetus for widespread transitioning. The diminished attendance at regular Church worship and an ageing priesthood visually signify its fragility and the reality of transition.[108]

Bayside was my first experience of parish ministry. It was formative for me. I met people who were seeking a deeper spirituality than weekend worship. Some began to meet regularly together in smaller groups for reflection and to support one another. This interested me greatly. My interactions with them, and what I was learning, were already laying a foundation for what was to follow for me.

A few years after my new appointment, in early 1990, I sat down with a few people from the parish of St John the Evangelist, Ballinteer, in the south Dublin suburbs. Our task was to prepare a series of presentations for Lent and host them within the parish in a way that would impact the spiritual sensitivities of all who might participate and engender a spirit of community among them. I was also anxious to cast it with an evangelising impetus, as I had seen a widening gap between church worship and everyday living, and I wished to bring faith and culture into dialogue.

108 At the same time, I do not wish to understate the vast amount of creative, energetic ministry that is part of almost every parish.

In late 1989, I learned of the possibilities of the parish cell system of evangelisation towards the renewal of parish life when I heard a short presentation from Don PiGi Perini during a retreat/seminar that I attended.[109] He spoke about the parish at Sant'Eustorgio, Milan, where he was parish priest, being committed to evangelisation. It now had almost a thousand small faith communities (known as parish cells), because each community in its commitment to evangelise multiplied and formed new ones. This multiplying and missionary method made a deep impression on me, and greatly influenced the format and expectations of the programme we were preparing.

I was familiar with Charismatic Renewal and involved as its national Catholic chaplain in Ireland for almost twelve years. I had experienced it at a personal level as 'a current of grace',[110] and knew of its life-changing impact upon me, upon individuals and communities throughout the world, and among people of different denominations. This was a further influence upon our new programme. After much thought, planning and soul searching, the series we eventually rolled out was the beginnings of what later became known as *Inspiring Faith Communities*.

We were gingerly dipping our toes into a spiritual outreach and inviting all parishioners, while suspending thinking on who or how many might relate to the programme. Hence my great surprise as I witnessed the reaction of the on average fifty participants who attended each evening. They spoke about recognising Christ's active presence in their lives in a richer and more personal way. They claimed to have begun to take on a greater joy and responsibility for their faith. They were learning to live a more vibrant sense of mission. They wanted to tell other people where 'good food can be found'.[111]

109 Don PiGi Perini launched the parish cell system of evangelisation at Sant'Eustorgio, Milan, after his visit to Mgr Michael Eivers, who had pioneered the initial parish cell system of evangelisation at St Boniface's, Pembroke Pines, Florida. Sant'Eustorgio became the centre from which parish cells spread throughout the world.

110 Pope Francis, address at the 37th National Charismatic Convention, 1 June 2014, Olympic Stadium, Rome, when he said 'You, Charismatic Renewal, have received a great gift from the Lord. You were born of the will of the Spirit as "a current of grace in the Church and for the Church. This is your definition: a current of grace".'

111 St Teresa of Calcutta, when asked to describe evangelisation, is said to have responded: 'It is one beggar telling another beggar where good food is to be found'.

They enjoyed having time and space where they could share their questionings and insights about God. As they did so, they formed strong bonds with their fellow participants and were eager to help and support one another.

Little did we think that our initiative, tentatively entered into, would have far-reaching consequences. The programme has changed during the intervening years due to the experience and feedback of people who have benefitted from it. It was run in a variety of parishes and adapted by parish teams to deliver specific objectives. It has proved to be a launching pad for small faith communities, for *lectio divina* and faith-sharing groups. It has been especially helpful when adapted as a programme in training parishioners for various ministries and initiatives. I know where one parish team, for example, decided that every parishioner would be visited in their homes, and this programme was used as a central component in training volunteers to articulate their faith and undertake this task. A number of parishes employed it to train ministers of the word, helping them to become familiar with the scriptures as words of life for themselves, and to deepen their faith in God whom they came to know as worthy of proclamation.

I know of one parish where all the members of the pastoral council attended *Inspiring Faith Communities* together. This changed the way they related to one another. Their times of prayer became more spontaneous. Scripture became an open book, which carried the 'sound' of God's voice. Members grew ever more attentive to his presence and word among them as their wisdom, guide and fulfilment. Their agenda became more mission centred, and focused on relating God's word to the circumstances of daily living and parish life. This emphasis helped replace the previously held 'democratic' or 'hierarchical' models of Church. Members no longer experienced themselves solely as individuals, called to meet expectations – of themselves and of fellow parishioners – or to undertake initiatives and events for fellow parishioners. Rather, they felt called by God, as his pilgrim people within their parish, to bear fruit (of community) in his name.

During each of my parish appointments since 1989, *Inspiring Faith Communities* has provided the catalyst for the launch of parish cell communities. I observed that it awakened faith for participants and gave them a sense of belonging. It facilitated recognition of the stirrings of God's love in their hearts, and for many a genuine faith conversion. It led people to a newfound curiosity about their relationship with God and the feeling of being 'reborn' in him. In seeking understanding and meaning, it led people to scripture as God's word, and to conversations with others who had somewhat similar experiences. They had fallen in love with God. This changed them. It gave them new perspectives and interests, and called them to make new decisions about staying in love with God and living in a way that attracts others to him.

At this juncture, the launch of parish cell communities made imminent sense. Indeed, they emerged almost spontaneously with a little encouragement, discernment and leadership. Parishioners had tasted something that brought them life, that kindled their spiritual longings, and awakened them to the richness of gospel living. They were seeking more of what they had experienced.

A New Initiative Is Born

In Ballinteer, the impact of the first programme upon individuals was such that twenty-eight people wished to explore further. They verbalised two great hopes. Firstly, that there would be spaces, supports or methods that would nourish, deepen and form what they were coming to know as real and life-giving. Secondly, that training would be provided to help them live and share faith in their relationships with others, especially with their children, families and the parish community. Much discussion and discernment followed about what would be most beneficial. As a result, four small faith communities (parish cells) formed.

As word spread, other parishioners were attracted and quickly began to gather with them. Within three years, thirty-one such faith communities had formed – some for adults, others for youth and a few for children. Every two weeks, these communities met in homes throughout the parish, with an average of ten people in regular attendance at each. I know that now, almost thirty years later, many of these communities continue as a leaven of faith, community, service and mission throughout the parish. The unexpected birthing of these communities, their spontaneous implanting within the fabric of the parish, and the rapid interest in them on the part of so many parishes throughout Ireland led us to deem that here was a moment of grace, a movement of God's Spirit, which deserved our best efforts in its nurturance.

The Parish Cell Experience

Many parishes around the world and throughout Ireland have adopted parish cells as a vision towards parish renewal. In doing so they are 'earthing' and giving shape to evangelisation in the concrete setting of parish life. They adopt them to form and make disciples. Parish cells are small faith communities of four to twelve people who normally meet in the informal setting of the homes of participants. Then, through reflection on scripture, listening to teaching, hearing each other tell stories of living their faith, and knowing they have the prayers and support of others present, they come to a deeper faith, enjoy community and depart eager to serve and witness. In this way, parish cells assist parishes, it can be claimed, to become 'a centre of missionary outreach', which Pope Francis names as his hope for every parish.[112]

The substantive purpose and orientation of parish cell communities is action that transforms and makes a difference. As is implied by their official name, The Parish Cell System of Evangelisation, they point towards evangelisation and mission. Their primary existence and *raison d'être* is to be at the service to others, namely, the evangelisation

112 *EG*, 28.

of individuals and of culture. Their purpose, and indeed their strategy, is to instil a conviction that moves people beyond their comfort zones to live faith in the hard places of family, neighbourhood, parish, business, community and leisure activities.[113]

Parish cell communities are places of communion. When real trust exists among all, they are inspirational centres. Many of the great stories, for example, that I hear from people who participate tell me that during times of great difficulty, these communities are for them places of hope, oases of peace and occasions of healing. People tell of times when something distressing happened to them or to a member of their family, which impinged upon them as a crushing pain. Much in their world had collapsed. All seemed bleak. At such times, the cell community shone glimpses of light that filtered through their darkness. These came in the form of support, in knowing that they were listened to and heard, in words of comfort, in hearing others verbalise their prayer for them, and in being helped in practical ways. People then knew they were no longer alone but that others were committed to journeying with them through difficult times, which brought them courage and healing.

Parish Cells Shaping Ministry

I am deeply thankful to Don PiGi, whose words awakened for me a new vision and method of parish renewal through small evangelising communities. This evangelising spark also gave shape to our first Lenten programme. Ever since, the development of parish cells and the nurturing of participants have greatly shaped my ministry as a priest. I now draw attention to three primary ways in which I have seen these influences at work for me.

Personal Conviction

Hearing people claim that a relationship with Christ had opened up for them was a deep inspiration for me. I had previously heard

113 This theme of engaging in the work of evangelisation is treated in depth in my previous work.

such stories. Now I was hearing them from people as they completed *Inspiring Faith Communities* and began to participate in parish cells. Their stories challenged me at a personal depth to move beyond faith being just a cerebral and neatly packaged intellectual exercise and to recognise the influence of God upon my daily living. At its core, it was a move from receiving and accepting faith and its categories to personal conviction. I was meeting a person. I was coming face to face with Jesus, as he revealed a divine loving in his life, passion and resurrection. In this, I intuited his offer of a relationship that would bring me new life and new possibilities. Indeed, I knew he was promising me 'life to the full' (Jn 10:10).

My narrow grasp of faith was being punctured by the stories and witness of those who had come to know God as transcendent, as, in the words of St Thomas Aquinas, the One who holds all things 'by essence, presence, and power', who at same time was someone intimately involved in their everyday living. People spoke about God as providentially caring for every aspect of his creation. They claimed to recognise traces of his presence and activity in nature, history and human affairs, and especially in the minute details of their lives. This insight, they claimed, was an act of God's grace. I found their witness challenging. I gradually realised that this too was a moment of God's spirit for me. A new vision of God and of my life in relation to him was opening up for me as gift, and not as the conclusion of reasoning abilities and efforts on my part. A deep personal conviction and enthusiasm about the sovereignty of God, his love, his word in the scriptures, in the Eucharist, in nature and in all that exists and happens, was forming in my being. This was to have a big impact on shaping my ministry. I felt drawn into attending to what I was experiencing. I also grew sensitive to what people were saying, and became eager to support them and to facilitate a personal faith in God for all whom I met.

I began to read widely about what people had said concerning seeing God's presence in everything and of his call to friendship. As

I did so, I noticed that what people were describing corresponded to the word 'ardour', as used by Pope John Paul II when he drew attention to the necessity for a new evangelisation that would be marked by 'newness in ardour, method and expression'.[114] 'Ardour', in his terms, refers to the enthusiasm and dedication that overflows in the lives of individuals as a result of an authentic encounter with Christ. This, he understands, is the first essential step without which there can be no genuine evangelisation.[115] As I recalled the stories of people who had participated in *Inspiring Faith Communities* and parish cells, and especially of their impact upon me, I realised that they exemplified an 'ardour' that propels people to evangelise.

Evangelisation
While I was already well aware of the evangelising possibilities of parish cells as a strategy for parish renewal from what I had heard from Sant'Eustorgio in Milan and St Boniface in Florida, I was now witnessing their impact upon individuals and upon parishes in an Irish setting. I was coming to appreciate at first hand that parish cells are agents of evangelisation.

The stories I heard were at times expressed with much sadness. The explanation ran something like: 'I have been a Catholic all my life and no one told me that this was possible.' On a number of occasions, anger against Church personnel accompanied this sadness in that they never seemed to have spoken of the possibility of such good news. For me, this remains a sad commentary on the people of faith who had evidently chosen to guard their great secret about the good news of Jesus Christ closely, or who, more likely, did not have the confidence or courage to share it with others.[116] It convinced me of the necessity to invite and empower all people who

114 Pope John Paul II, Port-au-Prince, Haiti, 9 March 1983.
115 See also *EG*, 120. Pope Francis would later use the words 'missionary disciples' to bring into focus that authentic faith involves at the same time being a learner at the feet of Jesus and reaching out in faith in the service of all.
116 I have seen estimates that show that fear prevents the majority of Catholics (up to 80 per cent) from inviting another to church or to a church-sponsored event. I have seen a survey finding that says that only about 2 per cent of Catholics invite another to trust in the person of Jesus and in his promises.

profess faith to undertake mission and to evangelise.

Listening to people tell of the impact of their new-found personal faith in Christ also questioned my assumption that every Catholic is conversant with the basics of faith. Rather, I came to see that poverty of understanding was widespread. I learned that not every person who claimed to be Christian knew of the core elements of faith. This was true for many who never, or rarely, attended church, but also for people who were in regular attendance. I listened to people's regrets that they had accepted assumptions, caricatures and memories as authentic Christianity, while being unaware of its power and of the personal nature of God, revealed in Jesus, as companion and source of life. Their new-found experience stood in sharp contrast to what they had accepted as normal Christianity. In recent years this gap seems to have widened significantly, and the models and images by which many people live serve only to distract from the basic realities of faith, Church and Christian practices, rather than openness to learn. For me, all this brought into focus the necessity for catechesis and teaching.

At the same time, the stories I heard convinced me of the central priority of the *kerygma*[117] in the initial presenting of faith, and also as a component in all teaching and preaching. In other words, primacy is to be given to knowing the Gospel as good news before celebrating it in worship, passing it on to others and living it out in relationships. This appears to be the practice during the first centuries of the Church's life. Kerygmatic presentations seek to facilitate a conversion of thinking and lifestyle through accepting the offer of Christ's love and friendship. Then follows the *didache*,[118] which refers to the instruction that assists understanding and living out what one has already experienced as faith. Teaching and catechesis thus build on and expand the initial kerygmatic conversion process. What people had said convinced me that this approach remains important

---

117 *Kerygma* comes from the Greek *keryssein,* to proclaim, and *keryx,* herald. It refers to the initial and central proclamation of the Gospel message.
118 *Didache* means teaching in Greek.

in leading people towards authentic faith. The importance of *kerygma* in the early Church is seen in the fact that the word appears many times in the New Testament.[119]

I observed that participants in parish cells engaged in evangelisation with a number of distinctive emphases, which I found new, refreshing and unique. Everyone seemed to be involved – to be on mission. All spoke readily and easily about their new perspective of God and about how they saw him influencing them in their everyday living. They seemed to live with greater joy, even abandonment. They had come to know a new hope, courage and trust in God's wisdom and love. They lived with a new freedom. For them, every event and encounter with another became a moment of divine providence, charged through with the possibilities and presence of love who is God and thus to be celebrated. They lived in expectation of God's intervening loving. It appeared to me that here I was witnessing the new 'ardour', which for John Paul leads to newness of method and expression.

For cell participants, sharing their stories is an act of loving. It is dialogue within a larger framework of hearing and responding to what is best for the other. One person tells another about what she or he finds life-giving at a personal level, and suggests that it is equally available to all. To evangelise, then, is to love. It is firstly and fundamentally a listening to another so as to be present as love demands. When told at the appropriate moments, telling one's story of faith invites another to include God's providential and intervening love as a central truth of reality, and as a spiritual scaffolding for hope, new beginnings, trust and love.

What struck me about this emphasis upon evangelisation was that it is within the possibility of everyone to achieve. It identifies the people who are the primary claim upon one's loving. Attentiveness to daily encounters, and especially when challenged to love, motivates it. The local as family, neighbour and friend becomes the principal arena of living faith and names one's missionary territory. In this, each

119 Mt 12:41; Mk 16:20; Lk 11:32; Rom 16:25; I Cor 1:21; 2:4; 15:14: 2 Tim 4:17; Titus 1:3.

individual evangelises as he or she goes rather than goes to evangelise. This was an important insight for me. Here was evangelisation that was relational, and expected as the normal task for all Christian believers. I had grown up thinking that evangelisation is what happens on the foreign missions. I later considered it to be programmes, events and initiatives, and the more heroic and dramatic they are the better they would speak to individuals and to our contemporary culture. Now, I was hearing from cell participants that evangelisation was neither organising activity on behalf of others, nor convincing them with information and debate, but rather about becoming friends who together share stories of life. This initiated a new pastoral approach for me, namely, helping people to know their faith story and to discern how and when to share it. Yes, parish initiatives and events remain important. They remain most effective when they form and deepen relationships and develop what Pope Francis calls 'a culture of encounter' with God and among people.

Parish cells are nurseries of creative evangelisation. They support the fragile flame of faith of each participant in putting down deep roots into the soil of God's Spirit, and in branching outwards to bear fruit in the Kingdom of God. Each cell is a community of people called together to pray, discern and reflect about how best to be a Christian presence through their daily relationships. They also determine what evangelising initiative God may be inviting them to undertake as a team. I know that many a creative insight emerges within the cell meeting about building bridges among people or taking on an initiative that bears much fruit. Parish cells are not a cosy cosseting of the comfortable, nor of the afflicted or distressed. They have a deeper purpose. The evaluation of meetings is in terms of how people beyond their cell are being served and loved, and how well the parish ethos is being impacted in communion with parish leadership.

Fundamentally, I witnessed a missionary spirit develop for parish cell participants, who are eager to pass on faith to family and friends. It was love in action. It communicated dignity and respect. It took time. It took patience. It was not first of all formulas and creeds but living in relationship to another and sharing stories. It was not shouted from the rooftops nor seen in newspaper headlines. There were no magic formulas, apart from a committed love and trust in God's timing. It was not an instant arrival at a destination but rather a step-by-step accompanying of another in the adventure of living.[120] And at times it meant resistances to be worked through with another depending upon God's wisdom and love. I also witnessed that as people grew in understanding mission, Church and parish, they volunteered time and expertise in a wide variety of services, which included ministry of the word, support of the poor and care of church buildings.

Community
Service as a way of life was stressed during my seminary training. Our vocation is to serve, we were taught. Ordination is for service. This was helpful. It laid the foundation for a spirit of generous service in our diverse appointments. However, I now see three weaknesses at work here. Firstly, there was little reference to whom we were first called to serve, with prayer largely demoted as a private undertaking. Secondly, it carried little reference to our clerical colleagues and lay members with whom we would serve. Instead, a rugged individualism was being instilled. Thirdly, faith tended to be presented as a private and individual enterprise.

Then I observed that as cell participants awakened to the omnipresence of God's love and guiding influence, they gravitated to others who had a somewhat similar experience. They felt a need to understand, discuss, discern and pray about what was happening to them. In this way, and almost unnoticed by themselves, community was forming. I saw, for example, that as people shared with one another during *Inspiring Faith Communities* programmes, very real and healthy friendships formed. Parish cells then continued what had

120 *EG*, 171.

begun and became for participants the locus where they witnessed that Jesus was fulfilling his promise: 'Where two or three are gathered in my name, I am there among them' (Mt 18:20).

As I observed the formation of small communities, I was delighted and challenged in equal measure. I took tentative steps to relate more personally with a few people, with whom I shared my enthusiasm, questions and need for prayer and direction. In this way I too was learning what participation in a small faith community meant. Then, hearing stories, scripture insights and spontaneous prayer, and encountering openness in giving and receiving, gave me a new appreciation of the richness, generosity and possibilities of the lived faith of lay people. This also gave me words to describe my own prayer and faith experiences. It renewed my confidence in seeing that faith 'works'.

The reality of a faith community became increasingly important to me. I noticed, for example, a deep sense of being church as God's people whenever I celebrated the Eucharist with those who had shared life within small faith communities. I also sensed a tangible awareness of God present among them, which they expressed in communal worship that was participative, and in an eagerness to witness to God in the world. I also had similar experiences while celebrating the sacraments of baptism, reconciliation and anointing the sick. These taught me the significance of the Church as *ekklesia*, as gathering, as the ones called out to gather as followers of Christ.[121] In this way, I learned that a deficit in a spirit of community is a fundamental weakness for Church communities today. Indeed, I now understand that the only way fully to appreciate our sacraments, and to hear scripture come alive as God's word, is within the context of relationships with others, while mindful of the wider communities to whom we are sent to serve.

The claim in scripture is that an engaging, interacting and

---

121 The term *ekklēsia* (church) is a Greek noun, which literally means 'the called-out ones', from the preposition *ek* meaning out of, and the verb *kaleo*, meaning to call.

participating faith community is the basic Christian witness: '... that they may all be one. As you, Father, are in me and I am in you, may they also be in us, so that the world may believe that you have sent me' (Jn 17:21). Fundamentally, we are called to share in the community of the Trinity, and when this is lived out in our relationships it will prove attractive and inviting for others to 'believe'.[122] C. S. Lewis echoes this fundamental reality and observes that the New Testament knows nothing of solitary religion.[123]

Today in Ireland, the survival of parish life where faith is lived, celebrated and expressed is at stake. We have already witnessed the virtual collapse of many parish communities. I am thinking of parishes where churches have closed as places of worship. More fundamentally, I think of those people who profess to be Christian in a given area but no longer gather together for worship or for religious purposes and hence no longer identify as a faith community. People may travel or commute elsewhere for sacramental celebrations, but no local public events mark and celebrate their belonging together in Christ. This means that the witness of community is lost. In my understanding, renewal of local parishes will re-emerge through its rediscovery, with perhaps only a small number of people taking on this shared responsibility for its life.

Small faith communities carry immense possibilities for advancing the quality of life of a new humanity. They provide spaces, for example, that nurture the heart's inherent longing for meaning and belonging, while giving and receiving. People engage with each other face to face and, in a humanely emotional way. they know and accept each other as persons. In this way, they alleviate the 'digital' loneliness that seems to be the experience of many people in a technologically oriented culture, which transfers volumes of information and business between people but often with little engagement between persons. They also provide

122 This theme runs through much of the writings of Donal Dorr, theologian, author and retreat-giver.
123 'No Christian and, indeed, no historian could accept the epigram that defines religion as "what a man does with his solitude". It was one of the Wesleys, I think, who said that the New Testament knows nothing of solitary religion. ... The Church is the Bride of Christ. We are members of one another.' C. S. Lewis, *The Weight of Glory*, 1945.

social capital, through their networks of friendships, which value each person for their own sake, and curb the tendency to hyperactivity in our culture with its emphasis on productivity and administration.[124]

My experience of parish cell communities attunes me to understand and to attempt to embrace the challenges of synodal co-responsibility in leadership within parishes. This proposes a radically new model of parish leadership, which no longer involves just a select few or a hierarchy, but invites all members of the community to take on pastoral and co-responsible leadership with the pastor.[125] Together, as a community of believers, they reach out to all, according to their ministries, charisms and giftedness. Ministry then becomes a function of grace and is received in a wide variety of forms as graced gifts from God in service of the community.

Gerry O'Hanlon, Jesuit theologian, claims that in the thinking of Pope Francis 'the Church for the third millennium must be synodal, collegial, an "inverted pyramid", in which the People of God are primary and the hierarchy in all its forms is there to serve the People in which the Holy Spirit is present'.[126] He then proceeds to give a flavour of what this means: 'It is a paradigm shift, a fundamental change which goes beyond even important adjustments to the existing model of Church. We are speaking here of a revolution, in its sense of a radical change to an existing structure.'[127]

Conclusion

In his poem, 'The Given Note', Seamus Heaney beautifully expresses and answers the great questions for musicians: Where does music come from? What is its source? How is it received? He does so by depicting the fiddler going out into the dark night and receiving his

---

124 William J. Bausch, *60 More Seasonal Homilies*, Mystic, CT: Twenty-Third Publications, 2002. 'It is incredibly easy to get caught up in an activity trap, in the busyness of life, to work harder and harder climbing the ladder of success only to discover it's leaning against the wrong wall.' Bausch cites Stephen Covey.

125 Pope Benedict XVI, in his address on 26 May 2009 when he opened the pastoral convention of the diocese of Rome on the theme: 'Church Membership and Pastoral Co-responsibility'.

126 Gerry O'Hanlon, *The Quiet Revolution of Pope Francis – A Synodal Catholic Church in Ireland?* Dublin: Messenger Publications, 2018, 9.

127 Ibid., 9.

tune from beyond the seen world. He explains:
> He got this air out of the night ...
> So whether he calls it spirit music
> Or not, I don't care.
> He took it out of wind off mid-Atlantic.[128]

The tune arrives from afar as gift to the fiddler who hears and plays it.

Heaney's description correlates with aspects of the nature of faith. I don't know how faith is communicated. I don't know how it arrives. I don't understand why some believe and why others with somewhat the same family influences do not. What I know is that when an individual deeply knows God's love, life changes. A new joy is visible. A new relationship with the world around them is born. A desire awakens to share stories of this good news with other people. This for me points to faith, given as gift, to infuse trust in God's goodness.

Neither do I know where parish cells come from. Yes, I know their history in the Catholic tradition in recent years: who first envisioned them, who pioneered them and how they spread worldwide. When asked I can tell what I know. However, I am also aware that I know little about them. I only know for sure that they are given us as gift from God. I have seen how *Inspiring Faith Communities* facilitates people to come to personal conversion through an encounter with Christ. I have seen parish cell communities nourish participants to take on an evangelising mentality, with a vision and strategy for the renewal and evangelisation of parish life. I find it remarkable that such simple processes so greatly influence individuals to grow confident in what they believe and to find words to share it with others. For this reason, I have come to see them as pointing to moments of grace and the work of the Spirit of God to awaken participants to the mercy and joy in God's love for themselves and for all whom they meet.

On 5 September 2015, Pope Francis addressed 5,500 cell representatives. The occasion was a celebration to mark the Church's

---

128 Seamus Heaney, 'The Given Note', *Door into the Dark*, London: Faber & Faber, 1969.

official recognition and approval of their statutes. Pope Francis urged them, 'Please do not forget that the statutes help you to walk on the right road but the thing that does the work is the charism! Do not let it happen that out of a desire to keep the statutes you actually lose the charism! Please nurture the cell charism.' The charism of parish cells, as a gift of God, he explained, is 'to make known the beauty of the Gospel to everyone'. He then linked closely the cell experience today and the Church at its beginnings when he said, 'meeting in homes to share the joys and expectations that are present in the heart of each person is a genuine experience of evangelisation which closely resembles what took place in the early times of the Church.'

I believe that facilitating a sense of the personal presence of Jesus in a person's life is a key pastoral priority today. It remains the greatest gift we can offer another. Nothing will bring greater meaning, hope, direction and peace. It arouses a curiosity and a desire, which opens to formation as a witness, and as 'a missionary disciple'. I see this evidenced in those who complete *Inspiring Faith Communities* and participate in parish cell communities. I hear it in their stories. I understand it in their questions for truth. I touch it in their love for one another and in their extending themselves while reaching out to befriend others, especially the most vulnerable.

I see in parish cells an expression of God's Spirit at work today. I welcome them as a stream of God's grace for our time. They have inspired me, surprised me, seized my imagination and given me many pilgrim companions. At times I, too, have been impatient, frightened, over-stretched, hesitant and unsure. But all the time I felt carried to risk trusting God's guiding wisdom, while ever thankful for the grace, vision and strategy of parish evangelisation that he has given. I am thankful that he has used many influences and stories to inspire my pastoral emphasis, and shape how I live mission and serve it through many and diverse ministries.